COMPASSIONATE RESPECT

A Feminist Approach to Medical Ethics and Other Questions

MARGARET A. FARLEY

2002 Madeleva Lecture in Spirituality

PAULIST PRESS
New York/Mahwah, New Jersey

COVER DESIGN BY LYNN ELSE

Library of Congress Cataloging-in-Publication Data

Farley, Margaret A.
    Compassionate respect : a feminist approach to medical ethics and other questions / Margaret A. Farley.
      p. cm.—(Madeleva lecture in spirituality ; 2002)
    Includes bibliographical references (p.   ).
    ISBN 0-8091-4115-9
    1. Medical ethics. 2. Christian ethics. 3. Feminist ethics. I. Title. II. Series
R725.56.F37 2002
174'.2—dc21

2002012195

Published by Paulist Press
997 Macarthur Boulevard
Mahwah, New Jersey 07430

www.paulistpress.com

Printed and bound in the
United States of America

CONTENTS

Margaret A. Farley holds the Gilbert L. Stark Chair in Christian Ethics at Yale University Divinity School. She received an M.A. in philosophy from the University of Detroit (now University of Detroit Mercy) and a Ph.D. in religious studies, with a specialization in ethics, from Yale University. She has authored, coauthored, or coedited five books, including *Personal Commitments: Beginning, Keeping, Changing.* She has published more than eighty articles and chapters of books on topics of ethical methodology, historical theological ethics, medical ethics, ethics and spirituality, and sexual ethics. In addition to her teaching, she is currently Co-Chair of the Yale University Interdisciplinary Bioethics Project; Director of the Yale Divinity School Project on Gender, Faith, and Responses to HIV/AIDS in Africa; and Co-Director of Sister to Sister: All-Africa Conference for Roman Catholic African Women addressing issues of HIV/AIDS. She is the recipient of nine honorary degrees and numerous fellowships and awards, including the 1992 John Courtney Murray Award for Excellence in Theology. She is a past president of the Catholic Theological Society of America and also of the Society of Christian Ethics. She has served on many editorial and advisory boards and national ethics committees. She has lectured in the United States, western Europe, Africa, and east Asia. She is a member of the Sister of Mercy of the Americas, Regional Community of Detroit.

COMPASSIONATE RESPECT **Compassionate RESPECT** Compassionate Respect COMPASSIONATE RESPECT **Compassionate Respect** Compassionate Respect COMPASSIONATE RESPECT **COMPASSIONATE RESPECT** Compassionate Respect COMPASSIONATE RESPECT **COMPASSIONATE RESPECT** Compassionate Respect COMPASSIONATE RESPECT **COMPASSIONATE RESPECT** Compassionate Respect COMPASSIONATE RESPECT **COMPASSIONATE RESPECT** Compassionate Respect COMPASSIONATE RESPECT **COMPASSIONATE RESPECT** Compassionate Respect COMPASSIONATE RESPECT **COMMPASSIONATE RESPECT** Compassionate Respect COMPASSIONATE RESPECT **COMPASSIONATE RESPECT** Compassionate Respect COMPASSIONATE RESPECT **COMPASSIONATE RESPECT** Compassionate Respect COMPASSIONATE RESPECT **COMPASSIONATE RESPECT** Compassionate Respect COMPASSIONATE RESPECT **COMPAS- SIONATE RESPECT** Compassionate Respect COMPASSIONATE RESPECT **COMPASSIONATE RESPECT** Compassionate Respect COMPASSIONATE RESPECT **COMPASSIONATE RESPECT**

*To my many students and colleagues at Yale University
who for more than thirty years have taught me
the meaning of a community of scholars.*

*And to the Sisters of Mercy,
who for more than forty years have shown me
the meaning of a community
of friendship and shared ministry.*

PROLOGUE

There is a strong relationship between Christian morality and the spiritual life, and therefore also between Christian ethics and spiritual theology. Because of this, I have thought it appropriate to address an ethical issue in this Madeleva Lecture series, even though I know that the series is importantly devoted to themes in what we generally call "spirituality." I hope that the relevance of my topic to this long-standing series will become apparent as I proceed.

I met Sister Mary Madeleva Wolff only once, and this was many years ago. It was enough for me to understand why this series has focused on spirituality and on women in so impressive a way. I was struck by the strength of Sister Madeleva's personality, the focus of her commitments, the wisdom in her perspectives, the poetic insight that shaped her understanding of the spiritual life, the grand scale of her inspiration regarding the future of women. Her contribution to the church and the world was and remains remarkable. I am honored to participate in this series and to follow a long line of Madeleva lecturers whose work has eloquently celebrated the legacy of Sister Madeleva.

I. THE PROBLEM

Beyond Compassion to
What Compassion Requires

Serious moral and religious obligations are always more complex than we think they will be. Ethical guidelines and theological concepts are stretched at every turn, even in our ordinary lives. What seems sufficient at one time in our personal and social histories is all too soon challenged by new situations or evolving and sometimes conflicting experiences. One conviction, insight, or internalized moral norm is countered by another, so that perplexity threatens to derail our efforts at moral discernment. If we are sufficiently uncomfortable with perplexity, we simply hold on to the insights that have served us well, and we avert our eyes from alternatives that might otherwise force us to change course.

Yet moral and religious insights have a way of growing or fading. They become deeper and more nuanced, or they are vulnerable to rigid, even fanatic, distortions of their original truth. Hence, when we probe apparent contradictions and unsatisfying ambiguities, sometimes we come to better insights, clearer perceptions of the content of our moral obligations. In this expanded version of my 2002 Madeleva Lecture, I want to explore two insights, two aspects of moral obligation, that have tended to threaten each other when held together in one ethical theory. The two I have in mind are compassion and respect, both serving as a linchpin in different ethical theories. Since the theories tend to diverge from one another, so do our understandings of respect and compassion. Yet common sense tells us they are not antithetical, and they may be profoundly related one to the other. I will argue that only if they are integrated, each requiring the other, will their full meaning be conceptually clear and practically useful in moral discernment.

Compassion and respect are important to our spiritual as well as to our moral lives. They are conducive to the widening of our hearts and minds in relationship to God and neighbor; that is, they are a means to love and to action. They are also constitutive of these relationships, part and parcel of the fabric of our love and the deeds of our love. Yet in our spiritual lives, too, compassion and respect are frequently separated, as if they did not always require one another to be truly what they are. While my central concern here is with the ethical significance of the relationship between respect and compassion, I want to suggest at least by implication that there is a need for them to be connected in the whole of our spiritual lives as well.

My exploration of the problems and the possibilities of understanding the relationship between compassion and respect will have four parts. Precisely because this problem may seem trivial in the light of common sense, I will begin by trying to clarify the theoretical and practical difficulties I have in mind. In order to do this, I will first offer, in this introductory chapter, an extended example of at least part of the problem. I will turn, in a second chapter, to its theoretical underpinnings. Nowhere do the theoretical difficulties become more stark than in current debates about approaches to medical ethics. And in no part of specialized ethics do concerns about contemporary feminist ethics find so ready a hearing than in contested areas of medical ethics. In response to these debates, I will offer a way to resolution, a way that I am calling "compassionate respect." In an effort to make my proposal plausible, I will attempt in a third chapter to reflect more fully on the religious, philosophical, and experiential meanings of both "compassion" and "respect." In so doing, my aim will be to show why and how they can only be what we believe them to be when they are, in a way, locked together. Finally, in what will be more of an epilogue than a full-fledged fourth chapter, I will try to show how, in the deepest sense of "compassionate respect," we do not avoid paradox. Yet without such paradox, we stop short of the central mysteries of Christian faith. If so, then we may also stop short of what is asked of us in our moral lives and what is offered to us in our spiritual lives.

A Case in Point

Compassion is a powerful response to human need and human suffering. Sometimes, however, an appeal to compassion can remain an empty appeal—not because the experience of compassion is empty, but because a recognition of what compassion requires is missing. Let me describe a potential case in point. It comes out of my experience as a participant in a White House Summit Conference for World AIDS Day, December 1, 2000. This particular year's conference was focused on the massive spread of HIV/AIDS across the world's South—that is, across nations, largely in the southern hemisphere, that are relatively (sometimes drastically) economically depressed and politically marginalized.[1] This conference was designed specifically to consider the role of religious traditions in response to the AIDS pandemic in these nations. Hence, the invited participants were, with few exceptions, leaders of religious traditions and faith communities in East and South Asia, Latin America, and (predominantly) Africa. Their presence in sizable numbers at this gathering represented a growing concern on their part and on the part of the coordinators of the conference for the role of religion in response to HIV/AIDS: Was religion, or would it be, part of the problem or part of the remedy for this most dire problem?

Imams, rabbis, patriarchs, archbishops, sheikhs, and many others came to the conference from the nations of the South to consider together what an effective religious response could be. One after another they spoke of how they had become aware of the importance of the problem of HIV/AIDS in their own geographical situations. One after another they articulated in terms of their own contexts the need for compassion. The shared experience of rising compassion was almost palpable. It included reports of compassionate responses on the part of faith communities to those vulnerable to and suffering from AIDS. Religious groups, it was noted, are caring for the dying and for the living, and they have begun to work at prevention and even advocacy for the needs of their people. At the individual, local, regional, national, and international levels, moving examples were given of new initiatives and already long-standing efforts. Yet implicit in the agenda of this conference was the recognition that more is asked of religious leaders and their cobelievers; the work has barely begun.

However powerful was the compassion and even the deeds of compassion described and expressed at this conference, many questions remained unidentified. Little was said about what compassion might directly require of religious traditions and their faith communities as interpreters of the pandemic and as transformers of some of its causes. The implication was clear that every kind of medical care is needed—for prevention, treatment, and ongoing support of the sick and dying. Care is needed, these religious leaders recognized, in ways that religious traditions can give and in ways that they cannot by themselves provide. The role of religious leaders includes, therefore, words and actions to move political and medical leaders to respond to the needs of the people. Religious caregivers can organize clinics; reach out to rural areas; support the few adults left who care for hundreds of children; lobby for desperately needed equipment, personnel, and funds; raise prophetic voices in calling the world to respond. All of these things appeared to be assumed; they were implicit in what compassion would require. If there were other specifications of what compassion would demand, they received little mention.

Hence, some questions seemed to be missing— questions directly related to the substance of religious traditions themselves. What, if any, has been the specific role of religious traditions and faith communities in shaping beliefs, attitudes, and practices that may have contributed to the spread of AIDS? Are new religious insights and teachings required in the face of the rising tide of the disease? What, for example, has been the impact of religious teachings regarding human sexuality, the status of women, and poverty? Whether at this conference or in any other forum in which such matters are discussed, few might deny that these questions are relevant to the remedies of worldwide AIDS. But few acknowledge them, and even fewer recognize what they entail. Responsibility for these questions remains significantly (though not solely) in the hands of those whose power has shaped responses to them through the centuries. At the White House Summit, the words of compassion were inspiring and uncontroversial. Words about sex and the status of women would have been controversial. And while churches and temples and mosques are better at addressing the role of poverty in the spread of this infection, an analysis of the intersection of gender, race, sex, and poverty would also have been controversial. Without such words, however, the requirements of compassion remained inadequately specified. Without them, there may have been no real recognition of what compassion in this context particularly requires of faith communities and the world religious traditions of which they are a part.

Worldwide AIDS and Understandings of Sexuality

Almost everyone agrees that some of the strategies necessary to prevent HIV/AIDS are actually available even in most countries of the South—strategies such as reduction in the number of sexual partners, increased condom use, treatment of other sexually-transmitted diseases, and safe injecting behavior. Yet there are few success stories on a national scale, Thailand and Uganda being perhaps notable exceptions.[2] Something is preventing concerted action. What is it? In part, at least, it is the silence that surrounds issues of human sexuality. Cultural expectations, frequently informed by and reinforced by religion, make questions of sexual behavior, marital fidelity, sexual orientation, and prostitution highly sensitive questions. Behind the silence surrounding these questions is to some extent a concern for privacy, a reverence for things central to human life, a belief that everyone already knows the answers to such questions. But to an even greater extent, the silence represents a deep shame that comes from the breaking of perceived taboos. This is true even if the taboos are customarily broken, as in the tacit acceptance of prostitutes as partners for men who must travel away from their wives and families in order to find work. When it comes to HIV infection, a whole chain of stigmatization may be falsely imposed on individuals, but it is no simple matter to dislodge it from the public mind. Stories abound, for example, of the exile or even stoning of married women infected by their husbands, and of unmarried women raped and infected by men who think that sex with virgins will prevent or cure their own infection by the AIDS virus.

One response has been to argue, quite rightly, that HIV infection can come from many causes— for example, injection of drugs. Hence, this infection can be dissociated from sexual behavior. Another response has been to reiterate strong moral rules that will guard against certain sexual behavioral risks. In many cultural contexts, neither of these responses has been very successful. HIV need not have any relation to sexual behavior, it is true, but sex is frequently implicated in the ways in which it now spreads so rapidly within and across so many nations. And ironically, the simple reiteration of traditional moral rules for sexual behavior has sometimes served only to heighten the shame and the stigma associated with HIV/AIDS, and to promote misplaced judgments on individuals and groups.

All of this is a wake-up call to religious traditions to the need to reexamine teachings about sexual morality and to consider ways to break the silence about sexual behavior. When these are traditions of world religions, it becomes a problem for us all. Teachings and practices are promoted not only in countries devastated by HIV/AIDS; they are the teachings of Christianity, Judaism, Islam, Hinduism, and Buddhism worldwide. We

11

do not hesitate to rethink our moral rules in other spheres of human life—social, political, economic spheres—when situations demand it.[3] All too often, however, a predominantly taboo morality is maintained in the sphere of sexuality—a morality whose power depends precisely on resisting critical examination, perpetuating fear and shame, and hence preventing either change or the deepening of traditional beliefs and rules. This is why the mere reiteration of long-standing sexual rules can appear moralistic, not responding to the deep needs of human persons or to their present experiences. This is also why an uncritical imposition of traditional rules can ignore the genuine requirements of justice and truth in sexual relationships. The AIDS crisis, if nothing else, tells us that this is no longer sufficient.

Does this mean that we can no longer offer a healing word, a word of promise and hope regarding sexual fidelity, responsible parenting, respectful intimacy? Quite the opposite. It means, however, that words carrying only harsh moral judgment are not enough, especially if our judgments cannot be sustained under careful examination. More than this, it means that we must all hear the voices of those—even within our own faith traditions—who speak of responsible uses for condoms, who witness to the possibility of just and responsible love between persons of the same sex, who challenge traditionally accepted patterns of multiple sex partners, who acknowledge that there are as yet no clear answers to issues of premarital sex, and who need us to help break the silence surrounding all of these questions. This is a task for faith communities in ways not open to others. What is the wise and healing word, the freeing word, the accepting word, the old yet radically new word, that we have to discern and to speak? Without it, without a transformation of insights into our sexual lives, prevention of HIV infection and slowing the tide of dying from AIDS will be unnecessarily and tragically limited. Compassion by itself cannot make up for clear-sighted recognition of what compassion requires.

Worldwide AIDS and the Status of Women

As the HIV/AIDS epidemic continues to burn its way across the world's South, women are at increasing and disproportionate risk of infection and death. They are also increasingly at the center of community, city, district, and national responses. Yet women's lack of economic, social, and political power remains a constraint in the prevention of AIDS and the care of those living with AIDS. Here, too, is a particular claim on faith communities, on religious traditions, that has not adequately been met. The United Nations may declare international years of women and pass resolutions regarding women, peace, and security. Particular countries may introduce measures to protect women from abuse and to assist them with their children. But if faith traditions do not address the gender bias that remains deep in their teachings and practices, changes for women will come too late to protect them from HIV/AIDS.

The sorts of bias that are relevant here include the continuing blatant exclusions of women from leadership and decision-making roles in churches, temples, and mosques. They also include the perpetuation of patterns of gender relations by which women are kept economically dependent on men, ultimately subservient to men, coerced into passive rather than active roles. Gender bias can also be more subtle than this—almost hidden from the general perception of both women and men, like the air we breathe and do not notice until a crisis such as AIDS makes us choke on it. Even when cultural pressures in some parts of the world have influenced faith communities to improve the status of women, the problem of gender bias remains a serious one for world religions as a whole—and hence for all who participate in them. From whatever part of the world the words of compassion for AIDS in the South arise, they cannot be effective without attention to this aspect of the problem.

Why do women bear a disproportionate share in the burdens of the AIDS pandemic? Without power over their sexual lives, they have little control over occasions of infection. Whether they are pressured into marriages not of their choosing, or as widows coerced into sexual relations with relatives of former husbands, or prevented from the knowledge and medical assistance necessary to limit their child-bearing, they live in a context where their subordination to men determines their health or sickness, life or death. Even in university settings, where education regarding sex and sexually-transmitted diseases is presumably available, massive numbers of women students become infected. "Sexual experimentation, prostitution on campus, unprotected casual sex, gender violence, multiple partners, and similar high-risk activities are manifested to a greater or lesser degree."[4] While men are also obviously infected through such practices, many of them are reported to say that they will not give up "their culture" because of AIDS—the culture whereby they are encouraged to have multiple sexual partners in order not to be considered "sissies."[5]

If educated women are at risk, the vulnerability of women increases exponentially when they live in small villages and rural areas without access to medical education. Here there is limited knowledge about AIDS, and mistaken understandings or silence about it generally prevail. There is little support for the use of condoms—which in many cases tend to be unaffordable, defective, or thought to cause rather than prevent HIV infection. Customary power differentials in gender relations make concerted action on the part of women almost impossible. As powerful as women may be in some spheres of their familial lives, they are often powerless, for example, in persuading male partners to engage in safe sex, or in refusing sex when it is demanded on traditional religious and cultural grounds. Given lack of access to appropriate health care, women are also rendered helpless when it comes to preventing the transmission of the virus to their newborn children.[6]

"In most societies, girls and women face heavier risks of HIV infection than men because their diminished economic and social status compromises their ability to choose safer and healthier life strategies."[7] Women are infected at an earlier age than men; a large proportion of new cases of HIV infection results from male perpetrated violence in the workplace, schools, and homes. In multiple situations of military conflict, women are systematically targeted for sexual abuse. Moreover, women experience discrimination in access to medical care when they are HIV-positive, and they are frequently denied the level of support from family resources that is given to men.[8]

It would be naive to think that cultural patterns that make women vulnerable to AIDS are not influenced by world religions whose presence is longstanding in their countries. Fundamentalisms take varied forms, but many of them are dangerous to the health of women. Women's own voices must be heard in order to trace the paths that lead to their infection. Leaders and participants in faith communities can no longer blindly support systems, their own or others, that ignore or underestimate women's needs, lack of access to care, and powerlessness to spare the lives of their children. Questions must be pressed about the role of patriarchal religions in making women invisible—even though women's responsibilities are massive, and their own agency can be crucial and strong. Such questions cannot be ignored if we are serious about a compassionate response to the crisis of AIDS.

Worldwide AIDS and Poverty

Religious and political leaders in the world's South have not neglected the connections between poverty and the spread of HIV/AIDS. In many ways, religious advocacy for the economically deprived and destitute has been and continues to be ongoing and strong. The relationship between poverty on the one hand and lack of medical education and care on the other—including tests for HIV infection and access to medicines—is everywhere visible. Yet rarely do faith communities expand their social analyses to the economic forces that drive sex industries or to the tragic consequences of worldwide discrimination on the basis of race, gender, geography, and class.

If there ever was a situation in which the principle of Preferential Option for the Poor was relevant and crucial, it is difficult to think of one more dramatic than the AIDS pandemic in the South. Identified first by Christian liberation theologians, this principle has its analogues throughout world religions and faith communities. Considered either as a strategic priority or a religious demand, it includes the moral imperative of turning to the margins of societies, communities, the world—to the outcast, the exploited, the forgotten, the shamed, the sick from whatever causes. Those who have been relegated or lost to the margins of life, power, resources are to be welcomed to the center where they can live in peace, flourish, determine their own destiny, participate in a shared life, and finally, like the rest of us, die with dignity amidst companionship and care. This principle offers a stark specification of what compassion must mean in the context of worldwide AIDS.

If religious traditions have anything at all to say to situations like this pandemic, they must speak about God (or whatever is for them ultimate) and about human responsibilities to one another in relation to God. To turn to the margins in order to bring all to the center is a requirement for those who believe in and speak about a compassionate God. In words and deeds it is demanded that we stretch our hearts and our homes to embrace those least likely otherwise to be respected, assisted, welcomed, and loved. This requires of affluent nations a radically new attitude to the South. It requires of world religions a sharing of international resources. It requires of countries in the South a new set of priorities in their own political and economic agendas.

All of us can say that we have sisters and brothers who are threatened with grave illness, or who are already sick unto death. Their lives are disrupted; their families are disrupted; their ordinary hopes are challenged in every way. And at present their numbers are growing. Insofar as these women and men and children share in our faith traditions, they have a special claim on us. Even if they stand outside of our communities of faith, they have a claim on us. The claim is on our compassion. Underneath the claim is a claim to our hope. Human persons are the sort of beings who cannot live without hope—without, that is, a sense of a future. Hope is to the spirit what breathing is to the body.[9] If compassionate offers of hope do not give the breath of life to our sisters and brothers in the context of our shared experience of the HIV/AIDS pandemic, then we must return to the sources and substance of our hope, searching within these for new springs of hope. For ultimately what is needed from us, and what is rightfully claimed, is *theological hope,* hope in God for us all. Such hope may be freed and visible only when we have done our work regarding new articulations of a sexual ethic, radical changes in relations between women and men, and everyday reaching to the margins so that all can be welcomed to the center. Short of serious efforts like these, compassion may remain impotent, and religious traditions will remain more part of the problem than part of any solution.

In detailing this problem for compassion in the context of worldwide AIDS, my aim has been to show that compassion needs to be normatively shaped, both as an attitude and as the generator of actions. The shape it requires is determined at least in part by the real needs of the persons to whom it is a response—in this case, needs for new understandings of human sexuality, new possibilities in gender relations, and new forms of distributive justice. I have not yet shown what all of this means in terms of the integration of compassion and respect. We have come, nonetheless, to the point where we may begin to see that compassion requires at its core not only love but truth—not only the passion of compassion but the truth that compels respect.

II. THE THEORY

If it is true that compassion requires normative shaping, then we must continue to probe what this means theoretically as well as practically. A likely context in which to explore the question further is the broader context of human sickness and health—moving from responses to HIV/AIDS to any and all experiences of medical need. This cannot and need not require us to address every form of disease or diminishment. My task in this chapter is not once again to identify particular requirements for compassionate responses to specific cases. It is, rather, to seek more light on the theoretical requirements that may apply in every practical situation that calls for compassion. The set of questions I am pursuing converges with some current developments in medical ethics. That is, a concern for compassion and its norms is parallel in many ways to debates in contemporary Western medical ethics about the relative adequacy of, on one hand, what is called an ethic of care and, on the other hand, what is identified as an ethic driven primarily by respect for individual patient

21

autonomy (or by any principles other than the principle of beneficence). Hence, although I seem now to be taking quite a different tack from the one with which I began, I believe that the lines of inquiry in the previous chapter and in this one will eventually come together in recognizable ways.

Medical Ethics and Its Discontents

Medical ethics as it has developed in the past thirty years now faces sharp challenges regarding its adequacy and appropriateness.[10] Its emphasis on ethical principles is criticized for the failure to incorporate concerns for character development or moral virtue. Its near absolutization of the principle of respect for individual patient autonomy is everywhere critiqued for indifference to beneficent concerns for the well-being of patients. As a medical ethic based on rights, it is pitted against proposals for a medical ethic based on responsibilities. Overall there is a growing concern that these kinds of dichotomies in approaches to the ethical provision of health care have themselves become counterproductive, or at the very least frustrating, for those who care a great deal about medicine and its responsibilities to the sick.[11]

The role of religion, or theology, in medical ethics has waxed and waned and seems now to be waxing again (a matter of serious import for our concerns here regarding ethics and spirituality, compassion and respect). But for medical practitioners, it must sometimes seem as if religion enters ethics today as one more competing voice in already conflictual situations.

What is needed is to move beyond the debates regarding the importance of autonomy *versus* beneficence, self-determination *versus* well-being, rights *versus* responsibilities, principles *versus* contexts, action guides *versus* development of character. In order to do this, I will propose an approach in which these polarized methods and values become mutually necessary and inseparable—an approach that I will try to articulate as both a principle and a disposition which I am calling "compassionate respect." This should clarify my treatment of the HIV/AIDS pandemic in the previous chapter and provide some theoretical base for the overall considerations of this volume. Since feminist ethics has been a key player in discussions like this, I will explore in particular the problems and possibilities of its contributions. In the following chapter, I turn to the question of what it might mean to look to religious as well as philosophical traditions not primarily for their conclusions on very specific medical ethical issues, but for their accumulated wisdom regarding compassion and respect.

Since many of the challenges to three decades of developing medical ethics take the form of critiquing the central place given to respect for individual autonomy, it is useful to formulate the problem in terms of the relative values and the potential intersection of autonomy and concern for patient well-being.

Autonomy and Beneficence: Principles in Tension

Fairly standard medical ethics, as it has unfolded since the 1960s, uses a relatively small number of concepts to evaluate ethical options in a clinical context. The list of these moral concepts usually includes individual autonomy (as applied to the patient), nonmaleficence (refraining from harming a patient), beneficence (the positive promotion of patient welfare), and distributive justice (fair allocation of limited medical resources).[12] The list also includes several other concepts derivative from these central ones—concepts such as truth-telling, confidentiality, fidelity, and rights of privacy. When these concepts are formulated into ethical principles or guidelines for moral action, they become the principle of autonomy (shorthand for the obligation to respect a patient's wishes and choices), the principle of nonmaleficence (the injunction not to harm a patient unjustly, which can include the fuller obligation to prevent and remove harm), the principle of beneficence (the obligation positively to help patients, to contribute to their well-being by remedying illness or injury, alleviating suffering, caring even through the process of dying), and the principle of justice (the obligation to distribute goods and services, as well as necessary burdens, justly). Other concepts are also lodged in principles, as for example the prohibition against deception, the obligation to respect patient rights to privacy and confidentiality, and faithfulness in the covenant between medical providers and their patients.

There has been general theoretical accord in medical ethics that the four major ethical principles of autonomy, nonmaleficence, beneficence, and justice carry in the abstract only prima facie weight. Which one will have priority when they conflict in a clinical context is not predetermined by an abstract ranking of their importance; none of them is considered by itself absolute; each has relative significance until its meaning in relation to a particular case is determined. Nonetheless, among these few principles, autonomy has enjoyed pride of place for more than a quarter of a century. It was given early impetus by the 1971 publication of Paul Ramsey's landmark book, *The Patient as Person*.[13] Since then, American medical ethics has accumulated a history marked by concerns first for research ethics and then clinical ethics; developments in case law and in moral theory; high visibility of the work of national commissions on bioethical questions; patients' rights movements; and so forth. Through all of this, the principle of autonomy has become so important that it is sometimes expressed as the principle of respect for persons.[14] In other words, the central ethical requirement to respect persons is frequently considered identical with the requirement to respect the autonomy—the self-determining, self-governing, decision-making capacity—of persons.

More recently, however, the principle of autonomy has come upon hard times. Its pride of place in biomedical ethics is seriously challenged. There are a number of important reasons for this. Some of them are simply new developments in moral theory: for example, a new preference for inductive reasoning over what some consider the deductive application of principles to concrete contexts; new critiques of exaggerated individualism and a correlative revival of interest in the importance of communities; postmodern skepticism regarding the integrity of a human self and the possibility of any real individual freedom; late twentieth-century reactions against what is considered the overly rationalistic function of ethical principles—today sometimes disparagingly called "principlism."[15] Added to these theoretical turns against the primacy of the principle of autonomy, there have also been disillusioning studies of the limited effectiveness of procedures for obtaining informed consent in clinical contexts.[16]

More importantly, clinical experience has compelled questions about the moral limits of the principle of autonomy, especially when it functions to

override seemingly serious concerns of nonmaleficence and beneficence in relation to patient care.
An obvious but somewhat ironic example is patient
decision making regarding refusal of resuscitation
in cases of cardiac arrest. Against a system that, for
reasons of efficient benefit to patients, made car-
diopulmonary resuscitation (CPR) almost auto-
matic whenever any patient's heart stopped
beating, the right of patients to say no was institu-
tionalized in Do Not Resuscitate (DNR) orders.
Now, however, new questions have arisen about
whether or not such a decision is indeed always the
right of the patient (or the patient's surrogates),
depending on her or his medical situation. That is,
there are cases where CPR appears to make no
medical sense whatsoever; in such cases, it may be
unethical to assume or to offer CPR as a possibility
for a patient—to be chosen or refused.[17] Concern
for the well-being of a patient may in these
instances render patient autonomy moot.

In most cases of patient refusal of proposed
treatment (a right of refusal now largely protected
by law), autonomy continues to hold sway. There
are other kinds of cases, however, where patient
(or family) choice is not about refusal of treatment
but about patient (or family) request, or even
demand, for a particular treatment. Whether or
not patient autonomy here trumps other considerations is less clear, especially when the treatment

being requested appears to offer no benefit to the patient and may even cause harm.[18] The provision of such treatment may contradict medical professional commitments and integrity. Here the question is whether patient autonomy includes more than the right to refuse treatment, more than the right to participate in decision making about treatment; whether, that is, it stretches to include a right to demand treatment when medical opinion is against it. Frequently these are the cases that come under the rubric of "medical futility"—a contested term, to be sure.[19] Important court decisions have centered around such cases, where medical professionals believe that continued treatment—including support of basic life functions such as breathing, taking in nourishment and water—holds no benefit for a patient.[20]

A primary focus on autonomy has also seemed counterproductive in the care of elderly patients. While age in itself is not a legitimate reason to ignore or negate the importance of free decision making on the part of a patient, it is a common experience of persons as they grow older that their sphere of autonomy diminishes. Dependence on others grows as capacities become limited. Overall, in the care of the gravely debilitated elderly, an emphasis on the principle of autonomy—while in some cases and in some respects still extremely important for responsible care—has served to reinforce cultural myths about individual independence as the basis of self-worth. When autonomy is narrowly construed in terms of total self-reliance, personal preference and self-assertion, it can compound the burdens of frailty and sickness that are experienced in varying and often increasing degrees.[21]

Finally, it is not infrequent in clinical settings today for caregivers and patients alike to lament the fact that a preoccupation with autonomy has tended to focus medical ethics too much on individual case quandaries and too little on the overall structural and organizational problems in the delivery of health care. Not only does autonomy thereby overshadow concerns for beneficence and nonmaleficence, it also obscures the more and more serious problems of distributive justice.

Advent of an Ethic of Care

Feminist theorists have for longer than most bioethicists been concerned about some of the issues I have been describing. What has developed more generally in virtue ethics, communitarian ethics, postmodern critiques of Western ethical theories, and so forth, has had a particular focus in feminist thought, tied as it is to a movement for the well-being of women (and, for many feminists, a concern ultimately for the well-being of women and men and children). What has come to be called an "ethic of care" has experienced (in the words of Alison Jaggar) a "spectacular rise to fame and fortune" in feminist theory and beyond.[22] The first formulation of this ethic came as a result of the empirical studies of Carol Gilligan beginning in the early 1980s. On the basis of these studies, Gilligan argued that there are two quite different moral systems, two independent approaches to moral questions. One, which she called an ethic of justice, is more likely (she said) to be the approach that men take; the other, an ethic of care, is more common in the moral reasoning of women.[23] Gilligan characterized an ethic of justice as concerned for individual autonomy, social contracts, a ranked order of values, principles—especially of fairness—and an emphasis on duty. An ethic of care she described as concerned with relationships between persons, cooperation, communication, an emphasis on responsibility, and caring.

Gilligan's theory combined well with issues raised by many other feminists, issues of what might be called "relationality" as distinguished from "autonomy." It took seriously many women's concerns for the needs of others, the sustenance of relationships, concreteness, particularity, respect for differences, and narratives (the stories of persons' whole lives, not only their discrete moments of decisional crisis). Ethics of care refused to make the primary approach to moral questions an abstract approach that falsely assumed commonality among

30

persons, ignored real inequalities, and presumed impartiality as the main arbiter of fairness.

Since the articulation of a feminist ethics of care by Gilligan, Nel Noddings,[24] and others in the 1980s, it did indeed rise spectacularly in fame and fortune—and not only generally in feminist ethics but particularly in bioethics, feminist or otherwise. Even the hardest of the hard-liners in favor of a so-called "principlist" approach and an emphasis on respect for autonomy have noted the importance of supplemental considerations of caring. Yet now, like autonomy, Gilligan's notion of "care" has come upon more difficult times. Critiqued first as gender-assigned (that is, further studies did not verify the identification of a care approach with women rather than men, and objections arose regarding the perpetuation of gender stereotypes), there has grown also a reluctance to accept the inevitability or even desirability of a dichotomy between the two approaches. Many feminists, in particular, insist that care by itself can be as morally dangerous as an absolute preference for autonomy.[25] This is graphically true in the clinical context. If, on the one hand, preoccupation with autonomy risks distorting our perception of the concrete needs of the patient for communication, companionship, assistance, and care—on the other hand, preoccupation with care, insofar as it fails to respect and even to foster autonomy, risks a return to the worst sorts of paternalism, mistaking harming for healing and the violation of bodily integrity for genuinely compassionate care. There must be a better way. Adding one to the other might do it, but perhaps not unless we can find out whether and how they combine.

The Requirements of Care

If there are moral and medical dangers attached to an ethic of caring, what are they, and what would limit or prevent the risk of such dangers? If care can be harmful or helpful, foolish or wise, mistaken or genuinely fitting, creative or destructive, what determines it to be one or the other? It must be that there are standards, criteria, measures for right caring, true caring, "just" caring. Care, in other words, has normative requirements; it must be normatively shaped, just as we saw above regarding compassion. But what are the requirements, and what might be the norms for true caring? In order to answer these questions, we need to consider more fully what "caring" is—in the sense intended by those who speak of an "ethic of care" and in an extended sense that we might want to identify. Although it refers to a disposition, a virtue, an attitude, an affective element of character, it is also used as a transitive verb. One "cares" in the sense that one provides needed assistance, pays attention to the concrete needs of another, and responds to those needs in some way. Within the meanings of care, then, we can distinguish a disposition for an affective response, the affective response itself, and the actions that express the affective response. We have therefore the caring individual (someone whose moral development is characterized by a disposition to care for others). We have the care that she or he experiences in response to others (the affective affirmation of those to be cared for).[26] And we have the deeds of caring (the actual taking care, assisting, helping another in ways that meet the other's needs).

If this is what caring is, what it aims to be and to do, then its requirements will include whatever will actually allow it to lead to the assistance of the ones who need care.[27] If we are mistaken about the concrete reality of those for whom we care, then both our affective response and our caring actions can take mistaken forms. In the long run, our very disposition for caring may be distorted so that it becomes more of a vice than a virtue. To illustrate with examples outside the medical context: If I care for my children only because I see them as appendages to me, only as the bearers of my name, or the fulfillers of my ambitions, they are in an important sense justified in saying that I do not really care for them and that what I intend as actions of care toward them are mistaken and harmful. Or if I care for them in relation to me as my beloved children, but I also care for them in a way befitting who they are as persons in themselves, I may still not care for them adequately or well. If, for example, I am quite obtuse when it comes to understanding their genuine needs, I may injure them when I provide for them what I have imagined they need, or wanted them to need, or projected onto them as needs that are more accurately my own. Similarly, in a medical context, my care for a patient may go awry if I do not pay close attention to the patient's history, diagnosis, prognosis, wishes, and established relationships.

It begins to be clear that the requirements for right and true caring are determined by the concrete reality of those for whom we care. The norms for right caring are lodged in the real needs of the real persons to whom we respond out of care. Yet normative matters are more complex than this. Since caring is a way of relating, its norms of obligation will include not only the reality of the one to be cared for but also the reality of the one who cares (the capabilities and limitations of a caregiver in terms of, for example, time, ability, and competing commitments). Moreover, since the reality of both the one cared for and the one caring includes their relationship, the norms for true caring will, in addition, depend significantly on the nature of the relationship—that is, whether it is familial, professional, a relationship between strangers or between friends, and so forth. All of this is true however much it must be nuanced in terms of the limits of our perception and understanding, or the changeableness of the reality we seek to understand and affirm. Insofar as we have knowledgeable access to "reality," true care will respond with actions that are needed, appropriate in a relationship, and possible.[28]

If we focus for now on the one who is in need of care, what content can we give to the formal principle that care must be fitting in terms of the concrete reality of this person? In a medical context, the principle translates easily into the requirement of responding to the need of a person in terms of her medical condition. To ignore this, to consider it distractedly, or to assess it negligently (and as a result, mistakenly) leads to bad medical care. Alternatively, to pay close attention, to bring to bear all of one's medical expertise and experience in an effort to understand the medical condition of this patient, will go a long way toward assuring good medical care. Yet perhaps more is at stake in good care than sheer medical diagnosis and knowledge of what is possible in the treatment of this particular condition. There is more to the concrete reality of this person than her medical condition, and guidance for her care may depend on more than expert assessment of what treatments to offer. To provide care for a person, whether medical care or any other kind of care, requires that she be understood as a person. She is, after all, neither a machine that needs fixing nor an animal of another species that needs healing in order to be restored to its particular form of health and well-being.

It is not necessarily to abstract from the concrete reality of this patient to consider what it means that she is a human person. Indeed, such considerations may illuminate her concrete individual reality and may reveal some of the central requirements of both respect and care for her as a person. Suppose we ask, first, what it will mean to respect her precisely as a person. Central to our response to this question (at least in Western culture) is that respect for her as a person means respect for her as an end in herself.[29] She is an end in herself because she has a capacity for free choice, for self-determination, such that it would violate who she is to incorporate her totally as a means into the agenda of another, whether of a caregiver or anyone else. This is what the principle of autonomy requires us to recognize and respect. Since the capacity for self-determination, or autonomy, is a central element at the heart of the reality of each person, no adequate or genuine care for a person can ignore it. Insofar as a particular patient is capable of exercising her capacity for free choice, respect for her requires that she be allowed and encouraged to participate (even to have the final say) in determining her medical care. However limited may be her present options, respect for her shapes a caring response to her as an end in herself.

But a person is an end in herself not only because of a capacity to determine her own destiny. There is a second element at the heart of what it means to be a person that is as primary as is autonomy and as important to our understanding of persons as ends.[30] This is the element that many feminists (and not only feminists) call "relationality."[31] We are who we are not only because we can to some degree make ourselves to be so by our freedom but because we are transcendent of ourselves through our capacities to know and to love. The relational aspect of persons is not finally extrinsic but intrinsic, the radical possibility of coming into relation, into union, with all that can be known and loved— including the possibility of union with other persons and with God, knowing and being known, loving and being loved. We are each a whole world in ourselves yet always beyond ourselves, "ends" because our center is at once beyond us and within us. We realize these capacities in concrete relationships formed in time and space. To respect a person as a person, then, is to respect her fundamental capacities for relationship as well as the relationships that are part of her concrete reality here and now. To care for a person adequately and genuinely as a person is to care for her in relation—in the context of the story of her relationships, past, present, and future.

Persons as we know them are also essentially embodied.[32] We are not disembodied freedoms and not disembodied partners in relationships. Insofar as our autonomy and our relationality ground as well as shape our right to respect, the obligation of respect for persons cannot be separated from the obligation to respect and to care for their bodies (or better, for them as embodied). Those who are medical caregivers do not need to be told this truth by feminists or any others. Respect and caring take account of the embodied needs of persons: needs for survival, for psychic security, health and fulfillment, freedom and relation. Embodied autonomy and relationality are not merely abstract ideas. All of the complexities of embodied human lives are part of the concrete realities we must try to understand if we are to respect persons and care for them truly. This means that respect for persons includes respect in terms of complex bodily structures, historical and cultural contexts, personal and institutional commitments, potential for many kinds of growth as well as actual maturation, individual and communal opportunities and responsibilities, failures and achievements, desires and hopes.

I have generalized about all of these dimensions of the human person, but another characteristic of persons is that each one is unique. The obligation to respect persons comprehends not only the obligation to respect individual autonomy but every other aspect of each unique person insofar as this is possible in a given situation and called for in a given relationship (not excluding the relationship each human may have to every other human, or each Christian to every other human). Insofar as care is a response to need, it is perilous to abstract from the intricate levels and forms of need that are part of any person's life at any given time. This is why the content of the obligation to respect persons provides the norms, the criteria for true caring.

Compassionate Respect

What "compassion" adds to "care" conceptually is both an element of stronger affective response and an assumption of more acute access to knowledge of the concrete reality of others. If care is the affective response to persons in need, compassion is this same response with the added notion of "suffering with" the ones in need. We all know the reasonable and necessary cautions to caregivers about not being inordinately "emotionally involved" with those for whom they care.[33] We also know the factors and forces that prevent "suffering with"—noncompliance on the part of patients, ingratitude, even the apparent repulsiveness of some patients; and the fatigue, impatience, weakness, and humanly-limited generosity of spirit of all caregivers at one time or another. Yet at the heart of the various medical professions there lies not only the possibility but the vocation to some degree and some form of compassion. From the vantage point of compassion we can better understand the mutual relationship and inseparability of compassion and respect, justice and care, principles and persons, autonomy and beneficence.

Precisely because compassion involves a beholding of the value of others and a suffering with them in their need, it opens reality to the beholder; it offers a way of "seeing" that evokes a moral response. The suffering of others is one of the locations in human experience where, whatever our epistemological skepticisms, we do encounter the reality of others and ourselves.[34] Perhaps nowhere is this more evident than in the clinical context of medicine. Here the needs of persons are frequently dramatic. Sometimes they rival any affliction known to human persons. Bodies are consumed by pain and disease; minds and spirits, too, are assaulted by loneliness, fear, and despair. Long nights and days go by where the endurance of patients, families, and caregivers is tested. Infants and young women, old men and strapping athletes, the injured and the ill dwell in a world of waiting or a world in which the favored medical metaphor is battle for life and for health.

Other kinds of suffering and need also dwell in the spheres of struggle and hope that characterize human life. There is the kind that does clearly lead to new life, literally to birth, or to new strength and mobility, new forging of family ties, new hope in a shared future. There is the kind where, out of disaster, injury, unexpected crushing disease, the battle is won, the unexpected ensues, the sorrow and pain yield to joy and comfort all around.

The point is that suffering in some form, great or small, overwhelming or overcome, has the power to grasp us when we see it in others. It has the power to hold us so that we cannot avoid the reality of the sufferers or the reality of ourselves. Insofar as we genuinely behold it, it awakens in us a moral response—to alleviate it, ameliorate it, prevent it in others, or if none of this is possible, to companion and literally "bear with" the sufferer, in love and respect.

In the medical setting, not all suffering is paradigmatic in this way. But even when it is not like this, the response to persons in need frequently derives from or participates in our perception of dramatic needs. If we cannot always see so clearly the concrete reality of each patient, or if we do not respond affectively in every situation, we nonetheless draw analogies from our deepest experiences and our most penetrating insights.

To behold, or even to remember, acute suffering can, of course, just as well distance us from one another, dull our moral sensibilities and the acuity of our ethical discernment. Moreover, if care can be mistaken, sometimes it is because our perception and interpretation of suffering is false. Compassion gives us access to concrete reality, and it awakens in us a moral response, but respect, too, can sharpen the focus of what we see and keep our compassionate responses fitting and true.

Compassion and respect are, therefore, mutually illuminating, and together they constitute a way of seeing the concrete reality of those who are in need. Compassion sheds light on the individual patient in her concrete situation in all of its particularity and complex embodiment; it also illumines the situation of sickness, reveals the form of relationship needed between caregiver and patient, places in relief structural deficiencies in the providing of care. It is not blind to the vulnerability of need, the asymmetry of caregiving relationships, the ways in which freedom is for the sake of relationship, but relationship makes freedom possible. So, too, the norms of respect, in the affirmation of the well-being of others and ourselves, shed light on what compassion will require: the maximization of autonomy insofar as possible, the protection of bodily integrity in some significant sense, the provision of knowledge and competent care, fidelity to commitments, honor to personal stories and deeply human hopes.

Compassionate respect, compassionate justice—here is a framework for an ethics of medical practice that, while moving beyond the dualities of other frameworks and approaches, does so responsibly only by incorporating them in a structured discernment for response. It moves beyond the polarities of care and autonomy, care and justice, persons and principles by allowing the content of respect to provide the criteria of care—by, that is, requiring care to be respectful of embodied autonomy as well as every level of need in the person to whom care is owed.

III. COMPASSION REVISITED

If my argument in the previous two chapters
regarding the requirement of a normative structure
for compassion is at all convincing, we begin to see
why compassion needs to be joined to respect.
Having examined what respect means, and what
the principles of respect entail, it remains to
explore more fully the correlative question of why
respect needs to be joined to compassion. I have
suggested the significance of compassion for grasp-
ing our attention and for revealing the needs of
those who suffer. Yet the meanings of compassion
are richer and deeper than anything I have
described thus far. Without probing these meanings
it is unlikely that an ethic of compassionate respect
will be more than minimally intelligible. In addition, such probing leads us to the religious dimensions of the concept of compassion, thereby
opening our deliberations more explicitly to the
realm of spirituality. This chapter, therefore,
attempts three things. First, I will consider the place
of compassion within the teachings of world religions. This may also provide a way to see a place

for religion in contemporary medical ethics. Second, I want to explore some historical and contemporary philosophical accounts of compassion. In so doing, it will be useful to distinguish compassion from other concepts that are related but in the end quite different. It will finally not do to employ terms such as *compassion, care,* and *beneficence* interchangeably as I have tended to do until now. Third, at the end of this chapter I will try to retrieve Christian notions of compassion, sharpening them with the philosophical distinctions I will have made, and showing how they can be located at the heart of a moral response to human suffering.

Religion and the Role of Compassion

Whatever one's valuation of the importance of religion for our understanding of compassionate respect, it seems unreasonable not to take seriously the centuries of rich moral experience on which religious traditions can draw. All major world religions have endured as world religions, at least in part, because they have had something to say in response to the large questions in people's lives, including the question of suffering. Far from being completely irrational, religious traditions have helped to "make sense" of parts of our lives in relation to the whole, aspects of life that philosophy alone has not been able to fathom.[35] In so doing, they have given meaning to both ordinary and extraordinary experiences, and they have shed light on our responsibilities one to another.

It is true that religions offer sometimes quite different, even competing, answers to fundamental human questions. But this may not detract from their importance in discerning the meaning and requirements of compassionate respect. On the one hand, we need all the wisdom we can get, even if it does not perfectly cohere. On the other hand, for all of our proclaimed religious and ethical pluralism, we frequently find ourselves in a medical context with an already shared framework and already shared goals. It is rarer than we think it will be that competing religious worldviews, if they are adequately understood, bring us to an impasse in discerning our obligations of compassion and respect.

What wisdom do we find embedded in religious traditions, anchored in the past yet often also developing in the present? The list of resources relevant to an ethic of compassionate respect is long. It includes priceless insights into the meaning of community, the possibility of transcendence, the call to justice in the world, the role of human freedom, the place for self-sacrificial love, the hope for mutuality in relationships, our responsibilities one to another, the ways of liberating action as well as liberating surrender, the many meanings of suffering, the presence of the sacred where we least expect it to be.

Religious traditions at their best also bring wisdom directly to bear on the moral meaning of human desires, the requirements of human love, the paths to human courage and generosity. And they have a lot to say about compassion.

Despite the complexity and variety of beliefs and practices within (and not just among) particular religious traditions, it is possible to locate compassion near the center of them all. Here I can only suggest directions in which we may look. For example, in the traditions of Hinduism, suffering is importantly connected with desire, and its conquest is a conquest of desire. But one's actions in the present have consequences for suffering in the future. Good actions, those that will change the course of suffering, are ones that flow from compassion to all the world of sentient being, and that therefore embody nonviolence, noninjury toward all. More than this, good actions are the actions that work to benefit others in need. Such actions are exhorted not only so that one can achieve advancement for oneself (that is, better karma), but because the beings of the world are worthy of beneficent deeds.[36]

In the many strands of Buddhism, a goal of self-transcendence requires a process of gradual self-forgetting; but it does not require isolation from those who are suffering. Indeed, the further one progresses, the greater one may be able to respect others. And while, as in Hinduism, suffering is caused by attachment and desire, there is a strong requirement—central to the Four-fold Holy Truths of Buddhism—to care for the poor and the sick. More particularly in Mahayana Buddhism, the ideal is the Bodhisattva who, even after having reached the goal, does not cling to it, but returns to care for those in need. At the heart of these traditions are stories whose power to evoke and to direct compassion and courage is in many ways unparalleled.[37]

Judaism and Christianity both raise up compassion for those in need as a requirement for the human community and a command of God. Again and again the prophets cry out in the name of God: "Is not this the fast that I choose: to loose the bonds of injustice, to undo the thongs of the yoke... to share your bread with the hungry and bring the homeless poor into your house?....*Then* your light shall break forth like the dawn, and your healing shall spring up quickly...." (Isa 58:6–8) [emphasis added].[38] And the voice of Jesus is heard through the centuries, "I was hungry and you gave me food, I was thirsty and you gave me something to drink,...I was sick, and you took care of me" (Matt 25:35–36). For many Muslims as well, comprehensive mercy toward those in need is an ethical obligation. "Spiritual chivalry is showing understanding and compassion equally to what appears good and what appears bad."[39] In each of these traditions the recording and retelling of stories and teachings have been aimed at awakening in hearers what the narratives and instructions advocate and depict.

Believers are not only exhorted to compassion and respect in Judaism, Christianity, and Islam. They are given God's own character as a model and a motivation.[40] It is, say the prophets and the psalmist, an attribute of God to be compassionate and just. "Gracious is the Lord, and righteous; our God is merciful. The Lord protects the simple…[having] delivered my eyes from tears, my feet from stumbling" (Ps 116:5–6,8). Moreover, God enters into a covenant with God's people, and within this covenant offers a model of mutually obligating love. Human persons are to imitate the ways of God, and though the biblical texts suggest that "the ways of God are not our ways," God's ways are to be trusted as *more* just, not less, and *more* compassionate, not less, than the genuine justice and compassion to which people are called. On this same premise, the Talmudic rabbis admonish the people, "Be like unto God; just as God is merciful and gracious, so be you merciful and gracious."[41] "Just as God clothes the naked, attends the sick, comforts the mourners, and buries the dead, do you likewise."[42]

Christians find in Jesus Christ a model for relating to those who are marginalized, debilitated, and scorned. The gospels report Jesus' actions of reaching out to the poor, healing the sick who are otherwise shunned, and all the while teaching that "as the Father has loved me, so I have loved you," and "this is my commandment, that you love one another as I have loved you" (John 15:9,12). Here, Christians believe, is a revelation of God's desires in relation to humans and to the world. In the death and resurrection of Jesus there is further revealed not the glory of death but the possibility that no matter what counterforces emerge, compassionate relationships can hold. And in the traditions of Islam, mercy is an attribute of Allah that inspires and demands of believers the practices of justice, kindness, and generosity. In the Qur'an, God says, "Call upon me, I hear the prayer of every supplicant. So let each respond to my call" (Qur'an 2:186).

There is no dearth of such religious texts regarding compassion. When it comes to integrating compassion and respect (especially for human autonomy), the record is more ambiguous and controversial. The multiple levels of human need and myriad possibilities of human suffering in body and spirit, mind and heart, are well attended to by religious injunctions to compassion. Where to look, however, for an obligation of compassionate respect for human freedom is a contested search from the start. The history of religious thought is deeply etched with struggles over dogmas about divine will and human response, providence and fate, election and damnation, respect for cobelievers but not for those who are perceived to be outside the favored cohort. Religious political history is also replete with failures to respect the freedom of human persons, freedom not only to live in peace but to engage in diverse practices of alternate religions. We can look to religious revelation for requirements of compassion regarding human bodily and spiritual needs, but understandings of the requirement of respect for individual and group autonomy have been long in coming. But such observations can be misleading. For world religions do, after all, offer some important resources for respecting human freedom and responsibility—resources worth retrieving in the construction of an ethic of compassionate respect.

Indeed, there is a responsibility for one's own destiny in both Hinduism and Islam, even when the language is all about no-self, karma, or nirvana. In Judaism freedom is a prerequisite for obedience to the Law; and to oppress others, manipulate them and destroy their options, or violate their personal integrity, is to fail to offer compassionate respect. Moreover, it is to fail to enter into partnership with God to build a world where peace and justice can meet.

In Christianity, there are many interpretations of the meaning of human freedom, the reasons for personal autonomy. All of them bear searching if we want wisdom on principles for compassionate respect. Despite the difficult theological struggles in the history of Christian theology regarding a human capacity for freedom, the thread of human liberty and responsibility appears in this history from the beginning to the present. Although the massive contribution of St. Augustine, for example, supports both freedom and loss of freedom,[43] he remains as a voice in which Christians hear of liberty and responsibility before one another and before God. The conflicted Augustinian legacy passes through Thomas Aquinas with an even stronger affirmation of human choice.[44] And while the Protestant Reformers denied any role for freedom of choice before God, the historical consequences of their thought were all on the side of human freedom.[45]

In the twentieth century, there is no more significant Christian theology of freedom than the one developed by Karl Rahner. A Roman Catholic thinker, anchored deeply in the tradition of Thomas Aquinas,[46] Rahner described the human person as fundamentally called to a radical and free response in love for God and neighbor. In the heart of each person lies the capability of self-determination, of utter self-disposal, for better or for worse.

God's almost incredible offer of friendship, of mutuality in love, of unending life is an offer from divine freedom to human freedom. Two liberties can meet. "The theological concept of liberty is theological in the first place because it explicitly or implicitly includes the thesis that whenever there is a radically responsible, true freedom of choice, there is also a definite relation to God."[47]

Liberty of choice is not, according to Rahner, merely the "ability to do one thing rather than another, let alone the possibility of always being able to do the opposite of what one has done before."[48] It includes this, but much more. For it is above all the possibility of disposing of oneself in love, of determining one's own destiny. No wonder, then, that Rahner underlines the importance of freedom in contexts of illness and injury, and above all, in relation to the prospect of dying.[49] Liberty is to be maximized, as far as possible, in and for every patient. Since every choice an individual makes throughout a lifetime changes her, her final choice may be her most important, the fruit of what she has become as a person. Compassion for individuals, therefore, will include respecting their capacity for free choice.

We have in religious traditions, then, multiple resources for understanding the significance of compassion and its relation to respect. Yet many of the brush strokes from religion on these matters are extremely broad. They open for us the power of stories, the vast revelation of our lives in relation to God, the clear call to "suffer with" a whole world of human pain. They mediate for us the obligation to do the deeds of compassion, the deeds of care. It remains for us, however, to clarify these understandings of compassion in greater detail. Here, therefore, it is useful to turn to voices of philosophers, whose sometimes meticulous analyses also open for us the meaning of compassion.

The Philosophical Fortunes of Compassion

If religion has been good to compassion but ambivalent about respect, philosophy has been better about respect than it has been about compassion. Philosophers certainly have not ignored the importance of compassion, and this is especially true in the context of medicine. The ancient Greeks already drew lines of debate about whether "pity" should be nurtured or disciplined. The Hippocratic tradition called on physicians to practice their art with compassion toward the sick person who would otherwise be vulnerable in his dependency on the healer. Medieval philosophers favored the virtue of "mercy," though they tended to lodge it in a hierarchical order of human relationships. Immanuel Kant did not care much for any emotions when it came to identifying moral obligation, but David Hume thought "sympathy" was the fullest expression of human moral capability. Arthur Schopenhauer argued that "compassion" is the only legitimate motive for developing attitudes and shaping behavior. Contemporary philosophers have shown a new interest in questions of care and compassion.

Hence, the fortunes of compassion both rise and fall in the history of philosophy. This, however, has actually helped to clarify its meaning and to provide it with useful critical assessment. Perhaps the most important service that philosophers have provided for our understandings of compassion is to make distinctions among its potential uses and meanings. This has frequently taken the form of distinguishing it from other terms and concepts such as pity, sympathy, empathy, and mercy. The net result of making such distinctions has not been to give us one clear meaning for compassion, since the term continues to be used differently by different philosophers. Nor have we finally achieved an uncontested valuation of compassion, since it is still more important to some thinkers than to others. Nonetheless, all of this work on compassion has enriched both our understandings of its possibilities and our appreciation of its significance.

Andrew Lustig in his *Encyclopedia of Bioethics* article on "Compassion" pulls together distinctions frequently made between compassion and its "cognate notions."[50] "Pity," for example, is often compared unfavorably with compassion because pity is more passive; it stands outside the suffering of the one in need and does not move to alleviate the need. "Mercy" differs from compassion in that it appears to be condescending, not a response to someone based on equal status.[51] "Sympathy" implies an imaginative identification with the suffering of another, but like pity it carries connotations of impotence, and there is often concern among philosophers that sympathy overwhelms reason. "Empathy," on the other hand, seems to represent a more controlled response, one that does not incapacitate the one who feels it. "Care" I have already described as it appears in contemporary ethics of care; and I have distinguished it from compassion in that care does not always imply "suffering with" another, only concern for his or her well-being (and/or one's own well-being). "Benevolence" is a positive attitude toward and response to another, wanting the other's good. "Beneficence" is acting with benevolence, and as a principle it identifies an obligation to act to secure, affirm, and promote the other's good.

The point is, as I have said, not that we finally get one and only one meaning for compassion, but that we see the many meanings associated with it and within it. We also begin to achieve some vantage point for evaluating the importance and the moral worth of compassion. As for actual terminology, philosophers remain all over the place in their usage of specific terms. For example, while some philosophers use "pity" in its pejorative sense, others (for example, Martha Nussbaum) use it as a positive term, equivalent to what I shall take compassion finally to mean.

But what are the real problems that philosophers have had with compassion (or with its cognate concepts and terms)? Included among the key figures who have been highly critical of compassion as a moral response are the Greek and Roman Stoics, Socrates and Plato, Immanuel Kant, and Friedrich Nietzsche.[52] The Stoics thought, of course, that all emotion must be disciplined by reason; they were, therefore, suspicious from the start of an emotion like pity or compassion. But more specifically, they believed that suffering can be eliminated in the virtuous person by disciplining emotions—whether of sadness or joy. Hence, no truly virtuous person will suffer. Hence, also, compassion felt for persons who are suffering will be mistaken about its object. Only those suffer who deserve to suffer, and who do not therefore deserve any kind of sympathy from others. They deserve respect as human beings, but not sympathy.

This theory is continued in Plato's reports of the views of Socrates. According to Socrates, good persons cannot be genuinely harmed: "Nothing can harm a good man either in life or after death."[53] The reason is that good persons are self-sufficient; they will not suffer with any experience of loss.

Whoever sorrows over a person's loss is contributing to the false belief that this loss was undeserved or a bad thing in itself. Thus, the kind of grief engendered by watching tragic dramas is bad for society. "We may say that [a good person] is most self-sufficient for living well…[and] that it is least terrible for him to lose a son or brother or wealth or any other such."[54] Suffering is not important because loss is not important. Pity is a form of "softheartedness," so that "We should rightly do away with the dirges of famous men, and leave them for women, not the best women, either."[55]

Yet Plato's concerns for the moral limits of pity do not represent total refusal to accord value to sympathetic emotions. It might be fairer to say that his focus was on the distortions of pity, and on the vulnerability it brings both to the one in need and the one who responds. As Elizabeth Spelman argues, "The fact that [Plato] does not dwell on suffering, nor leave us with his own cast of tragic figures, hardly means Plato was not occupied, even preoccupied, with human misery."[56] Plato was not opposed to grief but to the ways in which we may be beguiled by it. "When you get grief wrong you get much else wrong too."[57] Grief, after all, can be seductive—so that we take pleasure in seeing someone else's grief, wallow in our own, nurture the "plaintive part of the soul" without concern for moderation. Like some expressions of anger, the words and gestures of pity and grief can increase rather than ease another's pain as well as our own. These, Spelman observes, were the worries that led Plato (and Socrates) to oppose the dramatization of tragedy.

Centuries later, Kant expressed skepticism about the role of "inclination" in discerning moral obligation. This could include the emotions of pity and compassion insofar as they might undermine a strict attention to duty. But Kant's real quarrel with compassion was not only this; it was his belief that compassion was often condescending, indeed an insult to the sufferer.[58] Moreover, he suggested, if I let myself become "infected" by the pain of another (through imaginative identification), and if the pain cannot be remedied by me, then all that I accomplish is to increase the evils in the world. Now two people suffer instead of only one.[59] This notwithstanding, Kant also argued that active sympathizing with those who suffer can be a moral duty. "Thus, it is a duty not to avoid places where the poor, who lack the most necessary things, are to be found; instead it is a duty to seek them out."[60] We should not, he after all maintained, avoid the pain of compassion, since it can help us perform benevolent actions that we might not be able to do out of sheer duty.

Nietzsche had further reasons for judging *Mitleid*—pity or compassion—as life-denying, productive of negative value. Like Kant, he thought that it succeeds in doubling the amount of suffering in the world, for pain is now felt by two. But more than this, pity is the response of the "small man" to the troubles of the "great man." "When the great man screams, the small man comes running with his tongue hanging from lasciviousness. But he calls it his 'pity.'"[61] Compassion can·be a good thing when it is a superior granting mercy to an inferior, since truly ennobling suffering belongs only to the powerful and strong. Nietzsche finally recommended compassion only when it is a kind of parental concern for the good of society as a whole.

Major philosophical problems with compassion, then, come down to competing views of the human person—views of human emotion, moral virtue, and the fabric of human relations. Rather than first addressing these directly, it is helpful to look at what contemporary philosophers of compassion have to say that is relevant to these problems. Of these philosophers, the most sustained work has been done by Martha Nussbaum. But I shall consider also the work of Lawrence Blum and Elizabeth Spelman.

Against the Stoics, Socrates, Plato, and contemporary liberal and communitarian philosophers, Nussbaum argues that emotion is a form of thought; hence, compassion is a "certain sort of reasoning."[62] It is not irrational, not blind, not mere impulse. There is no final opposition between emotion and reason, since emotion involves reason and belief. Other philosophers might say that emotion is "intentional," meaning that it is not only a blind feeling triggered by someone's suffering, but that it is a perception of something in an object that is able to be examined, understood, critiqued. When Nussbaum articulates what she calls the "cognitive structure" of compassion, she follows Aristotle (a known proponent of a close connection between emotion and reason and a supporter of the moral value of compassion).[63] Aristotle considered pity, or compassion, to be a painful emotion directed toward another person's misfortune or suffering. As such, it depends on three beliefs about the suffering of the other—that it is serious, nonculpable, and resonant with the respondent's own sense of possible similar suffering.[64] Hence, Nussbaum defines compassion as a "painful emotion occasioned by awareness of another person's undeserved misfortune."[65] The importance of compassion for Nussbaum is that it constitutes a central bridge not only between individuals but between the individual and the community.

Lawrence Blum's aim is to give an account of compassion as a moral phenomenon. Like Nussbaum (and Aristotle), he identifies a cognitive structure for this emotion, lodged in the object of compassion. The object is a person (or a being capable of feeling or being harmed) who is perceived to be in a "negative condition," suffering some harm, difficulty, or danger.[66] The harm must be relatively central to the person's life and well-being (Aristotle's condition of seriousness), though it is not necessary that the harmed person be aware of it. Compassion as a response includes a desire to relieve the other's suffering and a disposition to perform beneficent actions. It typically involves an "imaginative dwelling" on the sufferer's condition, an "active regard" for her good, a view of her as a "fellow human being," and emotional responses of some degree of intensity.[67] It is not a pathological identification with another, where there might be confusions of identity.

Elizabeth Spelman's work in *Fruits of Sorrow* is focused on how we form our attention to human suffering. Suffering is everywhere, and it makes complex claims on us. We therefore need to become critically self-conscious about the ways in which we "sort out, measure, and give shape to" suffering and our corresponding responses. Spelman's own project in this regard includes the problematization of certain construals of sufferers—namely, as subjects of tragedy, objects of compassion, and what she calls "spiritual bellhops" (carriers of experience that we are all too ready to appropriate).[68] Insofar as these construals can be distorted, so too can the emotional and practical responses they inform.

Like Nussbaum and Blum, then, Spelman bases her analysis and evaluation of sympathetic responses to human suffering on the conviction that these responses have cognitive structure. "We could not regard our emotions as very interesting facts about us—in particular, as deeply connected to ourselves as moral agents—if emotions were simply internal events, things happening to us like headaches or bleeding gums."[69] But if emotions do have a cognitive structure, then they can be accurate responses to objects, or they can be deformed. Deformation seems to be critically recognizable when a response contradicts what we otherwise believe about persons, or when our very beliefs about persons are subject to critique. Thus, what we call tragedy may allow grief to go awry (as in Plato's charges regarding the role of tragedy in ancient Greece); compassion may be corrupted and thereby reinforce injustice (as when women's concern for men fosters women's injustice to one another); appropriating the sufferings of others for our own benefit can perpetuate inequalities (as when white women analogize their pain with the pain of black women slaves). In each such case, we may be missing the core of the suffering involved, and we may be organizing our responses in ways that are detrimental to a world filled with unjust suffering, and to ourselves as moral agents.

Insofar as historical philosophical problems with compassion are bound up with views of human emotion, moral virtue, and human relations, we can find light for these problems in the writings of contemporary thinkers like Nussbaum, Blum, and Spelman. All three reject an oppositional understanding of reason and emotion. Emotion has a thought structure, and as such, it can be tested for adequacy and accuracy. This is what is at stake in my argument in the previous chapters regarding the requirements of compassion—requirements that can be specified in terms of principles of respect and in terms of wholeness of perception of the concrete reality of the one suffering. In chapter 1, my point was that responses to HIV/AIDS in African countries will be impotent if compassion cannot open to an analysis of the particular causes and occasions of the spread of AIDS. In chapter 2, my contention was that ethical approaches to persons and situations in a medical context need to incorporate both compassion and respect, each illuminative of the concrete needs of patients, families, and professional caregivers. Precisely because emotions have a cognitive structure, compassion without norms can be mistaken, corrupted, and miss the real needs of real persons. But norms without compassion can miss the sufferer altogether.

When we encounter persons whose suffering is serious, we are awakened by a new epistemological connection. We see in a new way because we respond affectively in a new way. The lens through which we behold persons is widened and sharpened by both emotion and reason, compassion and principles. These are mutually enhancing, like Aristotle's description of "sympathetic consciousness," a kind of "loving knowledge" and "knowing love."[70]

More than this, Nussbaum is right to argue that the experience of compassion constitutes a bridge between ourselves and others. Compassion in its fullest sense is not a standing apart from the one in need; it is a sharing in the pain and suffering of a need unfulfilled, an injury not healed, an injustice not rectified. What must be added here, however, is that compassion is not only a response to need. It is a response to a person, a positive good that is in some way injured, oppressed, ravaged by pain, or simply not yet whole. Care is the form that love takes when the beloved is in need. But this means that the first response is love. It only secondly modulates into care and compassion. This is, to some extent, what philosophers are pointing to when they say that compassion includes seeing the one in need as a sharer with us in humanity.

It is also what some philosophers imply when they maintain that the sufferer for whom we feel compassion is not culpable for his own pain, though we might want to challenge some meanings of this assertion. The Stoics were wrong to think that only the bad suffer, or that a certain form of moral discipline can remove the pain of some kinds of losses. On the contrary, it is surely true that no one's culpability can finally destroy what is basically worthy of love. But I will return to these issues in the section that follows.

Finally, what view of human relationships can sustain a theory of compassion where suffering is doubled or where mercy must simply flow from the superior to the inferior? The experience of compassion itself tells us of a pain we would not be without, and of a sharing of burdens that does actually in some way lighten the burden of each. And who cannot glimpse the truth that in some deep sense all suffering is the same, even though no suffering is finally the same? Suffering is the great equalizer, but compassion reaches up and down and across, assuring a kind of equal respect—the kind that is part of what compassion gives. Or at least part of what compassion can offer.

All of these matters may be easier to understand if we turn to a particular religious tradition. Because I know this tradition best, I turn here to some Christian understandings of compassion.

Be Merciful as God Is Merciful

In the final section of this chapter, my aim is to clarify and expand some of the issues raised throughout the chapter, but also to move perhaps more clearly from the sphere of ethics to the sphere of spirituality. As I said in the beginning, I do not consider these spheres to be wholly separate in any case, but here I will emphasize more of the latter than the former. My approach will incorporate some central theological presuppositions, without an attempt at either systematic grounding or explanation. Given the limitations of this present work, there is more that I will not do regarding Christian notions of compassion than I will actually be able to do. I will not, for example, critique a variety of Christian beliefs or practices that no doubt need the critical self-consciousness that Spelman has identified as so important.[71] I will also continue to bracket questions of the meaning of compassion, or mercy, in situations of offense and punishment, especially in the sphere of the law. I bracket this even though I consider particular understandings of forgiveness, human and divine, to be crucial to Christian faith and practice.

Let me begin with two texts from the Christian scriptures that set a central focus for what I want to say about compassion. The first is often referred to as the "Doubting Thomas" text. The second is the text in which the story is told of two of Jesus' disciples who asked to sit at his right hand when his reign was finally established. In the first, recorded in the Gospel of John, Jesus is appearing to his disciples after his resurrection (John 20:24–29). He had encountered the group earlier, but one of them, Thomas, was absent. When Thomas was told of the earlier appearance of Jesus, he found this not to be credible and said to the others, "Unless I see the mark of the nails in his hands, and put my finger in the mark of the nails and my hand in his side, I will not believe" (John 20:24). In the previous appearance, Jesus had shown his hands and his side to those who were gathered. Now a week later, the disciples are together again, and Thomas is with them. Upon entering the room where they have assembled, Jesus says directly to Thomas, "Put your finger here and see my hands. Reach out your hand and put it in my side. Do not doubt but believe" (John 20:27).

There have been many interpretations of this text throughout the years, most of them focusing on the obvious challenge to Thomas and his final coming to believe: "My Lord and my God!" I do not intend to modify or ignore the traditional interpretation, but I want to consider an aspect not always acknowledged within it. Thomas recognizes Jesus by touching his wounds. This is probably not an experience of compassion on Thomas's part, but only an amazed testing by him of reality. Yet this reality—what Thomas comes to see as Jesus—carries wounds that the disciples (including Thomas) had run away from at the time they were inflicted. The wounds have become the signature mark of the one who had loved them, been lost to them, and who returned with the good news of God's forgiveness, acceptance, and salvation.

But why the wounds? Why not recognize Jesus by his face? his stature? his voice? These wounds are somehow at the heart of the Christian gospel. They tell Thomas not only that this is Jesus whom he has touched, but that this is the God who came to be with and for them even in suffering and death. Pious sentiments, perhaps, but here is Jesus, with wounds eternally healed, still among them. Here is Jesus, who had predicted he would take on the pain of all humankind, among them. Here is Jesus, whose wounds must represent, then, the wounds of all humankind, still among them. Here is Jesus, the face of God for them.

The second text, Mark 10:35–39, helps to explain the mystery that Thomas and the disciples face. It narrates the exchange between Jesus, James, and John (and in one account, the mother of James and John) about a possible place for the two disciples in the reign of God to come.[72] One day in their travels together prior to Jesus' suffering and death, James and John approach Jesus (perhaps their mother is behind them; perhaps they let her ask the question for them, as in Matthew 20:20–21). They inquire unabashedly as to whether they may have positions of privilege and power next to Jesus.

Jesus' response both deflects the question and answers it in a way that they do not at this point appear to understand. He says, "You do not know what you are asking. Are you able to drink the cup that I am about to drink?"(Matt 20:22). Without comprehending what has been said to them, they answer, "We can."

The cup to which Jesus refers is without doubt a cup of suffering. "Father, if you are willing, remove this cup from me..." (Luke 22:42). It represents his own "passion" and death. Hence, he is asking the disciples whether they are able and willing to share in the suffering *he will undergo.* Yet the suffering of Jesus includes more than what might be his individual pain. The Christian tradition has long taught that the suffering of Jesus takes up into it potentially the suffering of all humankind. Appropriating the prophet Isaiah's words, Christians have believed that "surely he has borne our infirmities and carried our diseases" (Isa 53:4).[73] The cup, therefore, to be shared was and is the cup of Jesus which is the *cup that holds the suffering of all persons.*

Belief focused through the image of this cup includes more, however, than that the agony of Jesus encompasses the agony of us all. The cup indeed signifies human suffering in all of its forms—sickness and tragic accidents, aging and diminishment, miscommunication and disparities in love, failures and catastrophes great and small. Yet in the context of the passion and death of Jesus, the sufferings that are central to the image are of a particular kind. They are sufferings that are the *consequence of injustice*. They are the sufferings, therefore, that *do not have to be*. The suffering that results from violence and abuse, indifference and false judgment, exploitation and oppression, abandonment and cruelty is suffering that cries out for an end not in death but in *change*.

What shall we make of these two Christian texts in the context of our explorations of the meaning of compassion? First, the texts come to us not isolated or in a vacuum, but situated in a religious tradition with deep commitments to theological interpretations not only of the story of Jesus but of the story of all creation, its fundamental reality, and its history. Second, they allow us to address some of the specific questions regarding human compassion that have emerged in our philosophical considerations of pity and compassion. Compassion for Christians needs to be placed in the ontological and relational framework of a theology of mercy. With this framework questions of the nature of emotion, worthiness in the object of compassion, expansion of suffering when it is shared, and the place of suffering in relationships of equality can be addressed once again. I shift here to the language of mercy only because it is more prominent in the history of Christian theology, though I continue to hold together within it the concepts of compassion and care.

At least in some of its key Christian usages, mercy is love for those who are in need. It is the gift that fulfills the need of those in misery, as bread is mercy to the hungry, warmth to the ones who are cold, a word to the ones who are lonely. Mercy is, too, the giving, the action by which the gift is given—as in the act of bringing nourishing food, lighting a comforting fire, reaching out to speak to one who stands alone. Beyond the gift and the giving, but also within them, mercy is the love on the part of the merciful person that modulates into compassion and care. It is a love that moves one to the actions of mercy, the giving of the gift. Mercy is therefore gift and giving and love, but the gift and the giving are the expression of the love, and they have all their meaning from the love.

Not every love and gift is therefore compassionate or merciful. Only if the loved one suffers some misery, so to speak, does the love become mercy, *misericordia*. Mercy is love for the beloved insofar as she is in need; it is fully merciful when it "feels" the misery of the other as its own. In Christian understandings of mercy, the one who loves is in some sense transformed into the one loved; the lover relives the loved one's misery within her own heart. *Cor miserum,* she commiserates. *Cum passione,* she loves with an affective indwelling in the other, and is moved to express a compassionate love by alleviating the misery of the beloved. Because mercy is first of all love for one in need, and all that mercy gives is an expression of that love, then love itself is the most needed of all mercies, without which we are all most miserable. The love of the giver is not only the basis of the gift of the lover, it is itself the greater gift.

If mercy is love for the beloved in need, and love makes the misery of the beloved its own, then we cannot understand mercy unless we understand misery. Where the range of miseries or needs is understood too narrowly, the range of mercy will be restricted as well. There is a sense in which all creation is actually a "needing" creation.[74] Misery is not always to be identified with the experience of extreme pain of mind or body. It can be first of all an ontological fact, and only secondarily psychological. To *be* "miserable" is to be missing something, to be in need whether one is aware of it or not. An undiagnosed cancer, for example, is still physical misery of a sort. The individual who has never tasted the sweetness of beauty or learned to thirst for wisdom, is empty of something— whether knowingly or not. *To feel* miserable is to be aware of emptiness, of illness, of brokenness, and to experience the pain of such needs. A compassionate love is not dependent always on sharing the feeling of misery, but on feeling in some way the misery itself.

There is even a kind of need that persists after it is met, after what is missing or awry is filled or made whole. This is the kind of need that permeates created being; it is the kind of need that makes a creature precisely a creature. It is a subsistent need, constantly responded to by divine mercy. Creatures whose being is full nonetheless need always to be held in their being and in their fullness. To exist fully and happily for a created being is to participate in the being constantly flowing into it by the creative and utterly present knowledge and love of God.

With this we see the vast ontological framework in which at least some strands of Christianity have understood divine mercy. As Thomas Aquinas argues, for example, "In every work of God, viewed at its primary source, there appears mercy. In all that follows, the power of mercy remains, and works indeed with even greater force."[75] Everything that is remains touched by God's mercy, and is itself a mercy. To know the length and breadth and height and depth of the mercy of God is to see it stretch from generation to generation, from one end of the earth to the other, from past to future, from the edge of nothingness to the heights of creation, down to the very depths of every being. As the psalmist never tires of singing, God's mercy provides the bread that gives us strength, the wine that makes the face glow, the rain early and late; it heals the sick, comforts the lonely, illumines the darkness, hovers over and enters into history. Everything that pours into our being—all life, sensation, thought, affection, our very existence—comes at the hand of this mercy. It is in the love and power of such mercy that human mercy shares.

Yet there are problems with this cosmic metaphysical view of divine mercy, with this mercy that reaches to the largest and smallest beings in creation. The first problem is one we are reminded of almost every day. That is, if God is all mercy, then we must admit that there is a dread mercy as well as a joyful one. God is all light, and nothing but light can come from light (1 John 1:5). God is all love and nothing but love can come from love. But when all is said and done, there is still darkness beyond the power of our minds to penetrate. Illumined by faith, we may catch a glimpse of the light that appears as darkness, and see that there is a misery which is itself mercy. Yet the human heart cries out for the kind of mercy we so desperately need, and the ontological as well as revelational framework shakes, just as the sacred world of Thomas the Apostle threatened to collapse in the face of nothingness and hope destroyed.

The second problem is that no matter how intimate we believe God's mercy to be, traditional theologies have made it seem distant. Here we have compassion that may lack what we consider to be the heart of compassion—that is, passion. "Mercy is especially to be attributed to God, provided it be considered in its effect, but not as an affection of passion."[76] Concern for consistency in a theology of God has led to the denial of any suffering in God—any change, "defect," compromise of the logical entailments of infinity. "A person is said to be merciful [*misericors*] as being, so to speak, sorrowful at heart...as being affected with sorrow at the misery of another as though it were his own....[But] sorrow...does not belong to God."[77] The model for mercy, then, becomes one of love but not "feeling with" the beloved, and inequality appears to be intrinsic to relationships of mercy.

There are ways to address these problems theologically, but here I want only to turn back to the two texts with which I began this section. In the light of Jesus' response to Thomas, and to James and John, what can we say about the problems of compassion—in a divine model or in a human participation in this model? Beginning with the dread mercies that can overwhelm our belief in a merciful God, we can intensify the problem by listening to the critics (whether Friedrich Nietzsche or contemporary feminists and womanists) who charge that Christianity is preoccupied with suffering, and as such it is a religion for victims. It provides spirituality for weaklings, but it covers over the depths of inhumanity and the silence of God. Christianity in this view seduces its adherents, making them passive, docile, and resigned to surrender to the forces of evil. It sentimentalizes suffering by refusing finally to give it its due. The cross of Jesus becomes a symbol only of death; it leads to an obsession with death but not to a rejection of what is life-denying. If there is mercy in death, then all honesty about death is foregone.

But Jesus' manifestation to Thomas is not of a failed savior, reveling in the wounds he has borne. Rather, what Jesus reveals is life, and wounds forever healed; death can no longer be the last word, not for creation as a whole or for anything within it. And the cup offered to the followers of Jesus is not finally a cup of necromancy and pain, but a cup of covenant, signifying the promise of a merciful God who drinks, too, in order to overcome suffering and death. The cup, then, is not only a cup of suffering but a cup of love and of life. Misery in the heart of the merciful does not "double" the pain of the world; it holds it all together, so that hearts break together in the sharing of one another's burden. Thus are the burdens lightened and transformed. For there is a love stronger than death, a crucified love that does not turn away from swords of sorrow, and that goes forth unconditionally no matter what the forces of evil may do against it. The point of the cup and the cross is not death, but that relationships can hold.

Because Jesus is the revelation of God, we now know that God is not impassive or merciful "without heart." "Whoever sees me sees [the one] who sent me" (John 12:45). What we experience as awakening to the suffering of another, the need of another, is not less—but infinitely more—in the experience of God. Divine mercy is in its first instance creative and redemptive, but in its second instance it is like the human mercy it aims to engender—that is, it is a response to the concrete reality of the beloved. It is a response to what is good, what is lovable, what is held in being by God's love. It modulates into a response to what is needed, to the beloved in need. In so doing, divine mercy does not stand on status, but dwells among us, emptying itself for our sake. Superiority and inferiority are not intrinsic to the model of mercy that Jesus reveals. "As [God] has loved me, so I have loved you; abide in my love" (John 15:9). And "this is my commandment, that you love one another as I have loved you" (John 15:12).

No longer can we think that compassion goes forth only to the worthy, for Jesus has taken on the iniquities of us all. "Rarely will anyone die for a righteous person—though perhaps for a good person someone might actually dare to die. But God proves [God's] love for us in that while we still were sinners Christ died for us" (Rom 5:7–8). Common humanity, created goodness, yes: this calls for our love and compassion even as it did God's. But non-culpability, worthiness: if this were required we could never either give or receive compassion.

Misery held in the heart of mercy, passion in the heart of compassion, need not be blind. It can open our eyes to see as God sees, to behold what is lovable, to attend to what is painful, to recognize the requirements of compassion. Mercy, like love, must be "fitting"—true to the concrete reality of the beloved. It does not ignore need; it addresses need. It aims to accept, to heal, and to sustain. Like God's mercy, genuine human mercy is formed by respect for what God has made—for human freedom, relationality, embodiment, historical and cultural formation, uniqueness, and the potentiality of fullness of life in an unlimited future. Like God's mercy, genuine human mercy is made true by its justice. Mercy and truth, each informing and unleashing the other: this is the mercy that God invites and commands.

EPILOGUE:
COMPASSION AND PARADOX

While I have tried to show that care and respect, compassion and its requirements, belong together without contradiction or opposition, I would be less than honest if I did not acknowledge that some paradox remains in any attempt to integrate them completely. A full and complex principle of respect for persons must shape and discipline as well as unleash compassionate response to real persons in their concrete reality. Compassion itself draws us to persons, arrests our gaze and focuses it, so that we cannot pass by them in their need. Respect tells us what is required, what is just, in compassionate response. Compassion leads us within and beyond the requirements of respect. Yet as I have said again and again, compassion must remain "fitting," still true to the person in need.

The requirements of respect, maximal or minimal, provide what might be considered the asceticism necessary for compassion. They hold us to the obligation that compassion awakens, and they compel us to sustain compassion all the way into the actions that both respect and compassion require. Respect is the Cross for compassion, the sword to its heart that allows its life to pour forth. Such considerations go beyond clear ethical analysis and lead us into the mystery of relationships, human and divine.

Christians (and other believers as well) know a lot about paradox. They know that in this world there is no sorrow that cannot open to some form of joy, and there is no joy without some limit in sorrow. They know that there is no presence without some pain of absence, and there is a kind of absence that makes presence possible (as when Jesus said he must depart in order to be with us all days, or when Thomas touched the wounds of Jesus yet could not, any more than could Mary Magdalene, secure forever in one moment the kind of presence he desired). Christians experience relentlessly in the middle of their nights and days the paradox of the "already/not yet," the fulfillment that cannot be enjoyed without the necessary "discipline of nonfulfillment." They know the paradox of hoping for things unseen, but also hoping in things already seen (for they have hope in this world, yet also in another world—not separate, not yet fully together, but in continuity one with the other). Christians are also not unfamiliar with the paradox that "in the death of all hopes, hope can [still] surge up and conquer."[78] Above all, Christians believe in the paradox of a love that finds only when it is willing to lose, and a life that is Life only when it is willing to die.

In the deepest experiences of compassionate love, where divine mercy is known and received and then given, there is mystery unable to be encompassed by categories either of compassion or respect. In these deepest experiences, however, the requirements of compassion and the requirements of respect come together in the requirements of a just and truthful love.

NOTES

1. The term *developing nations* has been rejected by many who live in these parts of the world, simply because it is a misnomer. Many of these nations are prevented from developing by the economic and political policies of those in other parts of the world.
2. The reasons for relatively greater success in these two countries has less to do with the role of faith communities than with national political leadership. Yet this leadership depended on support from religious leaders, or it had to subvert some of the traditional religious attitudes and beliefs that presented obstacles to addressing issues of HIV/AIDS.
3. An example of this is the gradual but finally radical shifts in the Roman Catholic Church teachings regarding so-called socialism, or regarding religious liberty.
4. Michael J. Kelly, "Challenging the Challenger: Understanding and Expanding the Response of Universities in Africa to HIV/AIDS,"

quoted in *International Higher Education Newsletter,* Philip Altbach (Summer, 2001).

5. Rosinah Kelebogang, report delivered to the Project on Gender, Faith, and Responses to HIV/AIDS in Africa, Yale University Divinity School. Unpublished manuscript, August 23, 2001.

6. Controversies have raged regarding research in sub-Saharan African nations on limited regimens for transmission prevention. Moreover, even with the lowering of prices of needed drugs by United States pharmaceutical companies, medications and general health care remain out of reach for many women in the South.

7. United Nations Special Session on AIDS Fact Sheet (June 25–27, 2001), 21.

8. Ibid., 21–22.

9. This is a paraphrase of Gabriel Marcel's point in *Homo Viator,* trans. Emma Crauford (New York: Harper & Row, 1965), 10–11.

10. I first began working on these issues when I was preparing to give the 1998 Dobihal Lecture on Religion and Health at Yale-New Haven Hospital. What follows incorporates some of the ideas I articulated in that lecture, though it represents a major expansion and reworking of the issues.

11. See, e.g., Edwin R. DuBose, Ron Hamel, Laurence J. O'Connell, eds., *A Matter of Principles? Ferment in U. S. Bioethics* (Valley Forge, Pa.: Trinity Press International, 1994); K.W.M. Fulford, Grant R. Gillett, and Janet Martin Soskice, eds., *Medicine and Moral Reasoning* (New York: Cambridge University Press, 1994); Diana Fritz Cates and Paul Lauritzen, eds., *Medicine and the Ethics of Care* (Washington, D.C.: Georgetown University Press, 2001).

12. These are the four concepts that frame the most widely used textbook in medical ethics. See Tom L. Beauchamp and James F. Childress, *Principles of Biomedical Ethics,* 5th ed. (New York: Oxford University Press, 2001). So popular is this framework that its critics refer to it as the "Georgetown mantra," since it was first put in print when both Beauchamp and Childress were connected with the Kennedy Institute of Ethics at Georgetown University. Today's use of the four concepts and the principles that incorporate them as ethical guidelines goes far beyond these authors or any one institutional base.

13. Paul Ramsey, *The Patient as Person: Explorations in Medical Ethics* (New Haven: Yale University Press, 1971). A new edition of this now classic volume, together with commen-

taries by Albert R. Jonsen and William F. May, is from Yale University Press, 2002.

14. This is not without precedent in the history of Kantian ethics, but as such I think it misses a great deal of what Kant himself wanted to incorporate into moral theory. It also skews contemporary medical ethics in ways that I will address below.

15. See, for example, DuBose, Hamel, and O'Connell, *A Matter of Principles? Ferment in U. S. Bioethics.*

16. See, e.g., C. W. Lidz, A. Meisel, M. Osterweis, "Barriers to Informed Consent," *Annals of Internal Medicine* 99 (1983), 534–43; Alan Meisel and Mark Kuczewski, "Legal and Ethical Myths About Informed Consent," *Archives of Internal Medicine* 156 (1996), 2525; Paul V. Holland, "Consent for Transfusion: Is It Informed?" *Transfusion Medicine Reviews* 11 (1997), 274–85.

17. CPR was developed as a procedure to "resuscitate"—reactivate arrested respiratory and cardiac functions—in a narrowly circumscribed set of patients. These were otherwise healthy patients whose heart and lungs had stopped working because of electric shock, sudden heart attack, drug overdose, drowning, and similar events. The procedure came to be used, however, whenever anyone "died," whenever

anyone—even someone in the final stages of a terminal disease, such as cancer—underwent cardiac arrest. It is these latter kinds of cases that open the question of whether or not CPR should be offered or considered standard care for all.

18. I am referring here to cases where specific treatments are involved, ones that would ordinarily be provided if they are considered medically appropriate. There is, of course, the larger set of issues in the United States about a right to any treatment (right to health care) if one falls outside the pool of persons who either have insurance or are covered by public programs such as Medicaid. Here, unfortunately, there is not much role for individual choice on the part of ill persons; we have not affirmed their right to obtain what they choose, and their right to refuse treatment is indeed moot.

19. See, e.g., Albert R. Jonsen, "Intimations of Futility," *The American Journal of Medicine* 96 (February, 1994), 107–109; Lawrence J. Schneiderman, Nancy S. Jecker, Albert R. Jonsen, "Medical Futility: Response to Critiques," *Annals of Internal Medicine* 125 (October 15, 1996), 669–74; Paul R. Helft, Mark Siegler, John Lantos, "The Rise and Fall of the Futility Movement," *The New England*

Journal of Medicine 343 (July 27, 2000), 293–96.

20. For an early case surrounding questions of medical futility, see Steven H. Miles, "Informed Demand for Non-Beneficial Medical Treatment," *New England Journal of Medicine* 325 (August 15, 1991), 512–15.

21. See, e.g., Bartholomew J. Collopy, "Autonomy in Long Term Care," *The Gerontologist* 28, Supplement (June, 1988), 10–17.

22. Alison M. Jaggar, "Caring as a Feminist Practice of Moral Reason," in Virginia Held, ed., *Justice and Care: Essential Readings in Feminist Ethics* (Boulder, Colo.: Westview Press, 1995), 179. See also: Diana Fritz Cates and Paul Lauritzen, "Introduction," in Cates and Lauritzen, eds., *Medicine and the Ethics of Care,* xiii–xxxiv; Susan M. Wolf, ed., *Feminism & Bioethics: Beyond Reproduction* (New York: Oxford University Press, 1996); Christine E. Gudorf, "A Feminist Critique of Biomedical Principlism," in DuBose, Hamel, and O'Connell, *A Matter of Principles?* 164–81; Mary Jeanne Larrabee, ed., *An Ethic of Care: Feminist and Interdisciplinary Perspectives* (New York: Routledge, 1993); Helen Bequaert Holmes & Laura M. Purdy, eds., *Feminist Perspectives in Medical Ethics* (Bloomington: Indiana University Press,

1992); Claudia Card, ed., *Feminist Ethics* (Lawrence, Kansas: University Press of Kansas, 1991).

23. Carol Gilligan, *In a Different Voice: Psychological Theory and Women's Development* (Cambridge: Harvard University Press, 1982). See also Gilligan, "Remapping the Moral Domain," in T. Heller, et. al., *Reconstructing Individualism* (Stanford: Stanford University Press, 1986); C. Gilligan, et. al., *Mapping the Moral Domain* (Cambridge: Harvard University Press, 1988).

24. Nel Noddings, *Caring: A Feminine Approach to Ethics and Moral Education* (Berkeley: University of California Press, 1984).

25. See Margaret A. Farley, "Feminism and Universal Morality," in Gene Outka & John P. Reeder, eds., *Prospects for a Common Morality* (Princeton: Princeton University Press, 1993), pp. 183–84; Jaggar, "Caring as a Feminist Practice of Moral Reason," pp. 179–202; Kathryn Tanner, "The Care That Does Justice," *Journal of Religious Ethics* 24 (Spring, 1996), 171–91.

26. I do not want to imply that only individuals who have achieved some high degree of the virtue of caring can experience care and perform caring actions. In a full-blown account of this, I would want to distinguish onetime

(or a few times) affective responses of care, as well as actions of care that are infrequent in a person's moral life, from the wholeness, consistency, and relative ease in experiencing care and doing the deeds of care that would characterize someone with the virtue of care. My presumption is that stable dispositions for caring develop in individuals over time, but that experiences and actions of caring can both exist without the stable disposition and can foster the development of it. In other words, I would lodge my understandings of these aspects of care within a fairly standard Aristotelian and Thomistic theory of virtue.

27. This is a position that extends my previous arguments regarding a norm for "just love." See Margaret A. Farley, *Personal Commitments: Beginning, Keeping, Changing* (San Francisco: Harper & Row, 1986), pp. 80–84.

28. This obviously assumes an epistemological realism of a sort. My own view is one that might be called a "chastened realism," one that acknowledges the partiality of all knowledge and the influence of social constructions of meaning on all that we know, but that nevertheless keeps looking to understand things as they are, as best we can. Much of contemporary theory is against this, but when we are in the realm of medical care, we cannot afford

theories that do away altogether with a conviction that we must attend to concrete persons and their very real needs.

29. At least this is what we affirm about persons in the language provided us by Immanuel Kant in the eighteenth century. The insight that persons are "ends in themselves" is arguably available much earlier—certainly in the beliefs of Christians (and adherents of other religions as well) that each person is uniquely beloved of God and intended for an unlimited future in relation to God.

30. See Margaret A. Farley, "A Feminist Version of Respect for Persons," *Journal of Feminist Studies in Religion* 9 (Spring/Fall, 1993), 183–98. See also Margaret A. Farley, "Feminist Theology and Bioethics," in Earl E. Shelp, ed., *Theology and Bioethics: Exploring the Foundations and Frontiers* (Dordrecht, Netherlands: D. Reidel Publishing Company, 1985).

31. Margaret A. Farley, "A Feminist Version of Respect for Persons."

32. It is probably misleading to say that persons are "also" embodied. Embodiment is not an "add-on" to what we are. This is the point of what I go on to say about "embodied autonomy" and "embodied relationality."

33. For a remarkable new set of arguments in favor of emotional involvement on the part of medical practitioners, see Jodi Halpern, *From Detached Concern to Empathy: Humanizing Medical Practice* (Oxford: Oxford University Press, 2001). See also the constructive review of this book by Nancy R. Angoff, "Making a Place for Emotions in Medicine," *Yale Journal of Health Policy, Law, and Ethics* 2 (Spring, 2002), 447–53.

34. See Margaret A. Farley, "How Shall We Love in a Postmodern World?" in Society of Christian Ethics, *The Annual* (1994), pp. 3–19.

35. For a useful rendering of this claim, see Ronald M. Green, *Religious Reason: The Rational and Moral Basis of Religious Belief* (New York: Oxford University Press, 1978).

36. See Green, *Religious Reason*, 201–212; John McKenzie, *Hindu Ethics: A Historical and Critical Essay* (London: Oxford University Press, 1922); R. C. Zaehner, *Hinduism* (New York: Oxford University Press, 1966).

37. For a concise overview of religious meanings of compassion, see B. Andrew Lustig, "Compassion," in *The Encyclopedia of Bioethics,* ed. Warren T. Reich, rev. ed., vol. 1 (New York: Simon & Schuster Macmillan, 1995), 442. See also Green, *Religious Reason,* 212–46; Raymond Pannikar, "The Law of

Karma and the Historical Dimension of Man," *Philosophy East and West,* 22 (1972), 35.

38. This and all following biblical texts are taken from the The Holy Bible, New Revised Standard Version, Catholic Edition (Nashville, Tenn.: Catholic Bible Press, 1993 and 1989). (Italics are mine.) I note here also a recent work by James Keenan that provides a perspective on the Decalogue (and a Christian appropriation of the Ten Commandments) as God's gift in the form of a call and imperative to compassion. See James E. Keenan, *Commandments as Compassion* (Franklin, Wis.: Sheed & Ward, 1999).

39. This is taken from an eleventh-century Sufi "spiritual warrior," Ibn al-Husayn al-Sulami, *Book of Spiritual Chivalry,* quoted in Laleh Bakhtiar, "Becoming a Fair and Just Person: Sufism and Mental Health," *The Park Ridge Center Bulletin,* no. 25 (January–February, 2002), 7.

40. On this theme in Judaism, see Green, *Religious Reason,*127–28.

41. *Michilta d'Rabbi Yishmael* on Exodus 15:2. Quoted in Byron L. Sherwin, "Toward a Just and Compassionate Society: A Jewish View," *Cross Currents* 45 (Summer, 1995), 156.

42. Rabbi Hama bar Hanina, quoted in Sherwin, 156.

43. Augustine's early writings (for example, *On Free Choice of the Will,* and even the narrative of his own experience provided in the earlier books of the *Confessions*) clearly presume and take seriously the capacity for human choice. Nonetheless, as he begins to appreciate the depths of human sinfulness and the need for divine grace, freedom gradually drops out of his writings (see the path of his thought from *On the Spirit and the Letter* to, for example, *On Rebuke and Grace* and *On the Gift of Perseverance*).

44. See, for example, Thomas Aquinas, *Summa Theologiae* I–II.13.6.

45. What I mean by this is that although Martin Luther and John Calvin leave little room for an undamaged and operable capacity for human choice, the result of the Protestant Reformation was the advent of new belief in individual freedom—especially freedom of religion and of political self-determination. See, on the one hand, Martin Luther, *On the Bondage of the Will,* and John Calvin, *Institutes of the Christian Religion,* III.20–24. But on the other hand, note the influence of the Reformation on all of the political movements in the West.

46. This must be qualified, of course, to indicate that Rahner's introduction to Aquinas was through Joseph Maréchal, a revisionist Thomist who integrated insights from Immanuel Kant into his interpretations of Thomas Aquinas. Rahner was also influenced by Martin Heidegger and by his formation in the spirituality of Ignatius of Loyola.

47. Karl Rahner, "The Liberty of the Sick, Theologically Considered," in *Theological Investigations,* vol. 17, trans. Margaret Kohl (New York: The Crossroad Publishing Company, 1981), 101. For a fuller view of Rahner's theology of freedom, see, e.g., his *Foundations of Christian Faith*, trans. William V. Dych (New York: The Seabury Press, 1978), esp. Parts I and III; *Theological Investigations,* vol. 6, trans. Karl-H. and Boniface Kruger (Baltimore: Helicon Press, 1969), 178–96; vol. 18, trans. E. Quinn (New York: The Crossroad Publishing Company, 1983), 89–104.

48. Rahner, "The Liberty of the Sick, Theologically Considered," 102.

49. Ibid., 105–113. See also Rahner, "Christian Dying," *Theological Investigations,* vol. 18, 226–56.

50. Lustig, "Compassion," 440.

51. Sometimes "pity" is thought to have this element of condescension as well. Lawrence Blum

interprets it this way when he says that with pity "one holds oneself apart from the afflicted person...and from their suffering....That is why pity (unlike compassion) involves a kind of condescension, and why compassion is morally superior to pity." Lawrence Blum, "Compassion," in *Explaining Emotions,* ed. A.O. Rorty (Berkeley, Calif.: University of California Press, 1980), 512.

52. My interpretation of these issues draws upon the historical writers themselves but also on contemporary commentaries. I am particularly indebted to the following: Martha C. Nussbaum, *Upheavals of Thought: The Intelligence of Emotions* (New York: Cambridge University Press, 2001), esp. Part II; Nussbaum, "Compassion: The Basic Social Emotion," *Social Philosophy and Policy* 13 (1996), 27–58; Elizabeth V. Spelman, *Fruits of Sorrow: Framing Our Attention to Suffering* (Boston: Beacon Press, 1997), chap. 1; and Blum, "Compassion," 507–517.

53. Plato, *The Apology* 41D, in *The Last Days of Socrates,* trans. Hugh Tredennick (Baltimore: Penguin Books, 1957), 50.

54. Plato, *Republic* 387 DE, in *Great Dialogues of Plato,* trans. W. H. D. Rouse (New York: Mentor Books, 1956), 184.

55. Plato, *Republic,* ibid.

56. Spelman, *Fruits of Sorrow,* 16.
57. Ibid., 17.
58. Immanuel Kant, *The Metaphysical Principles of Virtue* 34–35, trans. James Ellington (New York: The Library of Liberal Arts, 1964), 121–23.
59. Ibid., 34
60. Ibid., 35
61. Friedrich Nietzsche, *Thus Spoke Zarathustra* III. The Convalescent 2, in *The Portable Nietzsche,* trans. Walter Kaufman (New York: The Viking Press, 1969), 330.
62. Nussbaum, "Compassion: The Basic Social Emotion," 28. This view of emotion, and in particular compassion, is also argued at great length in *Upheavals of Thought.*
63. See Aristotle, *Rhetoric* 1385–86, *Nicomachean Ethics* 1106b, and the whole of Aristotle's treatment of emotions, the voluntary and the involuntary, virtue, and so on.
64. Nussbaum, "Compassion: The Basic Social Emotion," 31ff. See also *Upheavals of Thought,* 306.
65. Nussbaum, *Upheavals of Thought,* 301.
66. Blum, "Compassion," 507–508.
67. Ibid., 509.
68. Spelman, *Fruits of Sorrow,* 1.
69. Ibid., 103.
70. Aristotle, *Nicomachean Ethics* IX, 9.

71. I think in particular of an earlier critique I made of Roman Catholic Church policies in the public form in the United States. See my "The Church in the Public Forum: Scandal or Prophetic Witness?" Presidential Address, *Proceedings of the Catholic Theological Society of America* 55 (June, 2000), 87–101. My concern was to challenge the church to move from its preoccupation with, for example, the abortion issue, to a more balanced distribution of personnel and resources directed to other issues of human well-being that are, indeed, on its political agenda. The issues I raised in this publication could well be pondered from the perspective that Elizabeth Spelman suggests when she writes, "Compassion, like so many of our other complex emotions, has a heady political life. Invoking compassion is an important means of trying to direct social, political, and economic resources in one's direction...." *Fruits of Sorrow,* 88.

72. I have previously explored this text and its relation to the issues I am raising here in "History, Spirituality, and Justice," *Theology Digest* 45 (Winter, 1998), 1–8; and also in "One Thing Only Is Necessary," *MAST Journal* 2 (Summer, 1992), 17–23.

73. While it is true that language such as this often refers not to suffering of all kinds but to the

suffering that is marked by moral fault, nonetheless a deep strand of Christian belief and piety maintains that in some way all human suffering (indeed, all the suffering of the universe) is taken up into the suffering of Jesus.

74. I am indebted for some of these formulations to the late Jules J. Toner, whose conversations with me on questions of divine mercy have, I am certain, left long-standing insights in my memory.
75. Thomas Aquinas, *Summa Theologiae* I.21.4. *Basic Writings of Saint Thomas Aquinas,* ed. Anton C. Pegis (New York: Random House, 1945), I. 228.
76. Aquinas, *Summa Theologiae* I.21.3.
77. Ibid.
78. Karl Rahner, *The Great Church Year,* ed. Albert Raffelt, trans. Harvey D. Egan (New York: The Crossroad Publishing Company, 1994), 165.

The Madeleva Lecture in Spirituality

This series, sponsored by the Center for Spirituality, Saint Mary's College, Notre Dame, Indiana, honors annually the woman who as president of the college inaugurated its pioneering graduate program in theology, Sister M. Madeleva, C.S.C.

1985
Monika K. Hellwig
Christian Women in a Troubled World

1986
Sandra M. Schneiders
Women and the Word

1987
Mary Collins
Women at Prayer

1988
Maria Harris
Women and Teaching

1989
Elizabeth Dreyer
Passionate Women: Two Medieval Mystics

1990
Joan Chittister, O.S.B.
Job's Daughters

1991
Dolores R. Leckey
Women and Creativity

1992
Lisa Sowle Cahill
Women and Sexuality